Macmillan Building and Surveying Series

Series Editor: Ivor H. Seeley
Emeritus Professor, Nottingham Trent University

Accounting and Finance for Building and Surveying A. R. Jennings
Advanced Building Measurement, second edition Ivor H. Seeley
Advanced Valuation Diane Butler and David Richmond
Applied Valuation, second edition Diane Butler
Asset Valuation Michael Rayner
Building Economics, fourth edition Ivor H. Seeley
Building Maintenance, second edition Ivor H. Seeley
Building Maintenance Technology Lee How Son and George C. S. Yuen
Building Procurement Alan E. Turner
Building Project Appraisal Keith Hutchinson
Building Quantities Explained, fourth edition Ivor H. Seeley
Building Surveys, Reports and Dilapidations Ivor H. Seeley
Building Technology, fifth edition Ivor H. Seeley
Civil Engineering Contract Administration and Control, second edition
    Ivor H. Seeley
Civil Engineering Quantities, fifth edition Ivor H. Seeley
Civil Engineering Specification, second edition Ivor H. Seeley
Commercial Lease Renewals – A Practical Guide Philip Freedman and Eric F. Shapiro
Computers and Quantity Surveyors A. J. Smith
Conflicts in Construction – Avoiding, Managing, Resolving Jeff Whitfield
Constructability in Building and Engineering Projects Alan Griffith and Tony Sidwell
Construction Contract Claims Reg Thomas
Construction Law Michael F. James
Contract Planning and Contract Procedures, third edition B. Cooke
Contract Planning Case Studies B. Cooke
Cost Estimation of Structures in Commercial Buildings Surinder Singh
Design-Build Explained D. E. L. Janssens
Development Site Evaluation N. P. Taylor
Environmental Management in Construction Alan Griffith
Environmental Science in Building, third edition R. McMullan
European Construction – Procedures and Techniques B. Cooke and G. Walker
Facilities Management – An Explanation Alan Park
Greener Buildings – Environmental Impact of Property Stuart Johnson
Housing Associations Helen Cope
Housing Management – Changing Practice Christine Davies (Editor)
Information and Technology Applications in Commercial Property
    Rosemary Feenan and Tim Dixon (Editors)
Introduction to Building Services, second edition Christopher A. Howard and
    Eric F. Curd
Introduction to Valuation, third edition D. Richmond
Marketing and Property People Owen Bevan
Principles of Property Investment and Pricing, second edition W. D. Fraser
Project Management and Control David Day
Property Finance David Isaac

Property Valuation Techniques David Isaac and Terry Steley
Public Works Engineering Ivor H. Seeley
Quality Assurance in Building Alan Griffith
Quantity Surveying Practice Ivor H. Seeley
Recreation Planning and Development Neil Ravenscroft
Resource Management for Construction M. R. Canter
Small Building Works Management Alan Griffith
Structural Detailing, second edition P. Newton
Sub-Contracting under the JCT Standard Forms of Building Contract Jennie Price
Urban Land Economics and Public Policy, fifth edition Paul N. Balchin, Gregory H. Bull and Jeffrey L. Kieve
Urban Renewal – Theory and Practice Chris Couch
1980 JCT Standard Form of Building Contract, second edition R. F. Fellows

Series Standing Order (Macmillan Building and Surveying Series)

If you would like to receive future titles in this series as they are published, you can make use of our standing order facility. To place a standing order please contact your bookseller or, in case of difficulty, write to us at the address below with your name and address and the name of the series. Please state with which title you wish to begin your standing order. (If you live outside the United Kingdom we may not have the rights for your area, in which case we will forward your order to the publisher concerned.)

Customer Services Department, Macmillan Distribution Ltd
Houndmills, Basingstoke, Hampshire, RG21 2XS, England.

Constructability in Building and Engineering Projects

Alan Griffith

Hong Kong Polytechnic University

Tony Sidwell

University of South Australia

MACMILLAN

First published 1995 by
MACMILLAN PRESS LTD
Houndmills, Basingstoke, Hampshire RG21 2XS
and London
Companies and representatives
throughout the world

Learning Resources
Centre

ISBN 0–333–58815–0

A catalogue record for this book is available
from the British Library.

10   9   8   7   6   5   4   3   2   1
04   03   02   01   00   99   98   97   96   95

Copy-edited and typeset by Povey–Edmondson
Okehampton and Rochdale, England

Printed in Great Britain by
Antony Rowe Ltd, Chippenham, Wiltshire

Contents

Preface   vii

Acknowledgements   viii

1 Constructability: Concepts and Principles   **1**

   1.1   Introduction   1
   1.2   Development of Concepts of Constructability   3
   1.3   Development of the Principles of Constructability   13
   1.4   Constructability: Stages of Consideration   22
   1.5   Benefits of Good Constructability   25
   1.6   Barriers to Implementation   26
   1.7   The Search for Better Constructability   28

2 Strategies for Constructability   **31**

   2.1   The Need for Constructability   31
   2.2   Project Aspects Influencing Constructability   34
   2.3   The Construction Process   36
   2.4   Constructability: Strategies for the Construction Process   40

3 Constructability in Conceptual Planning and Procurement   **42**

   3.1   Conceptual Planning for Constructability   42
   3.2   Procurement Options   44
   3.3   Traditional Contracting   45
   3.4   Design–Construct   46
   3.5   Management-Based Methods   64
   3.6   Design- and Management-Based Methods (Project
         Management)   74
   3.7   Constructability and Conceptual Planning and
         Procurement: Summary, Overview and Strategies   79

4 Constructability in Design   **85**

   4.1   Design Constructability   85
   4.2   Design Factors Influencing Constructability   86
   4.3   Constructability in Design   87
   4.4   Design Constructability: Summary, Overview and
         Strategies   102

5   Constructability in the Construction Phase   **106**

5.1   The Contractor's Responsibilities   108
5.2   Design Solution   110
5.3   Techniques of Assembly   111
5.4   Personnel Organisation   113
5.5   Site Organisation and Layout   115
5.6   Project Communications   121
5.7   Operational Control   122
5.8   Availability of Skills and Labour Resources   126
5.9   Constructability Case Study Examples in the Construction
       Phase   128
5.10   Constructability in the Construction Phase: Summary,
       Overview and Strategies   134

6   Constructability in Use   **138**

6.1   Maintenance – A Total Process Approach   138
6.2   The Requirements for Maintenance and Repair   140
6.3   Capital Project Management   142
6.4   Condition-Based Maintenance Management   146
6.5   Constructability and Use: Summary, Overview and
       Strategies   147

7   Constructability Case Studies   **151**

Case Study 1:   Multi-Storey Building: Shaftwall Construction   151
Case Study 2:   Arts and Entertainment Centre: Procurement   155
Case Study 3:   Reservoir and Pumping Station   159
Case Study 4:   Academic Facility: Steel Framed System Building   160
Case Study 5:   Multi-Storey Building Services: Fast Track Lift
                Installation   169
Case Study 6:   Historic Building Refurbishment   172
Case Study 7:   Local Government Public Service Building:
                Low-Rise Traditional Construction   174

8   Constructability: an Overview   **179**

Appendix: Glossary of Terms   181
Select Bibliography   182
Index   183

Preface

Constructability is 'a system for achieving optimum integration of construction knowledge in the building process and balancing the various project and environmental constraints to achieve maximisation of project goals and building performance' (Construction Industry Institute, CII, Australia); it can therefore bring real benefits for clients, consultants, contractors and users. It is an approach that links the conceptual planning, design, procurement, construction and user phases of a building or engineering project, enhancing both the logistical aspects as well as cost effectiveness.

This book provides a review of the concepts, principles and practices of constructability, at each stage in the total construction process, thereby illustrating how clients can achieve better quality of service, greater value for money, improved speed of delivery and greater economy.

Chapter 1 introduces the concept and principles of constructability, highlighting the potential benefits, identifying barriers to its implementation and indicating the way forward to better constructability in modern building and engineering projects. Chapter 2 develops the theme to place constructability as a concept within the building and/or engineering processes. Chapter 3 focuses on constructability in conceptual planning and procurement, reviewing the impact of different procurement routes on constructability. Chapters 4 and 5 concentrate on constructability considerations in the design and construction phases, while Chapter 6 looks at constructability in use and its direction towards the influence of maintenance and repair. Chapter 7 takes the concepts and principles identified in the preceding chapters and illustrates these in a series of constructability case studies in building, engineering, services and refurbishment. Chapter 8 concludes the work with an overview of the concepts, principles and practices of constructability within the total construction process.

The term 'constructability' has been adopted in this book because it is most widely accepted as applying to the total construction process. Where other authors or researchers have particularity referred to 'buildability', then this term has been used in context.

ALAN GRIFFITH
TONY SIDWELL

Acknowledgements

Appreciation is extended to the following for their involvement in this work: Professor Ivor H. Seeley, the Series Editor; the Construction Industry Institute, University of Texas, Austin, USA; the Construction Industry Institute, Australia, University of South Australia, Adelaide; all authors, respondents and collaborating companies who have contributed information and support.

1 Constructability Concepts and Principles

1.1 Introduction

Better value for money, improved quality of service and quite significant savings in both project cost and time are clearly possible through the detailed analysis not only of the individual phases of the total construction process but also of the interaction between those phases. In any building or engineering project, seeking improvement through the careful consideration of procurement, design, construction techniques and management approach should make implementation easier, quicker and cheaper. 'Constructability', in the broadest sense, embodies a conscious attempt to recognise in each constituent phase of a construction project that those facets can promote improvement both to that phase and also to the total construction process. Constructability identifies the opportunities for maximising the route of procurement, design input, design–construction collaboration and use and upkeep of the finished product. However, it must be emphasised that constructability is not a concept that should be invoked as an imposition; rather, it must become an implicit and accepted characteristic of the construction process, to which all the various construction professionals contribute. Furthermore, the use of constructability to reduce costs and simplify construction implies neither lower quality nor compromise in design.

A considerable body of opinion within the construction industry has suggested over many years that the traditional separation of the design and production functions within the construction process has been primarily responsible for the general lack of consideration given to the necessary and vital integration between project phases. Too often the propensity for improvement is lost because construction is thought of as little more than a routine production function almost deliberately separated from project planning and design. Fundamentally, the philosophy, systems and approaches traditionally in use do not lend themselves to the consideration of alternative designs, construction techniques and managerial procedures.

In addition, many construction professionals are not completely conversant in the use of innovative materials and components, do not perhaps appreciate the implications of design and/or engineering upon construction methods and generally may lack empathy for the demands of the construction process, in particular those that lie outside their own professional focus. Some construction professionals continue to use both ineffective techniques and somewhat antiquated management, perhaps for fear of change or owing

1

to a lack of understanding. R. Jortberg, chairman of the first task force on constructability for the Construction Industry Institute in the United States, says[1] that 'designers and engineers don't know what they don't know'.

He characterises them as existing in a system of parallel but discrete pipes with no interconnecting pipes to allow the crossflow of understanding. While in some building and engineering contracts the opportunity does exist to pursue constructability concepts, the plain fact is that in many building and engineering projects maximum opportunity for improvement is lost because insufficient thought and attention is paid to constructability.

The fundamental aim of research into constructability over the years has been to promote a greater awareness of those factors that can influence the design or the production process and, in so doing, improve the opportunity for the contractor to give the client better value for money. The main area of focus has been the relationship between design and construction, and the investigation of the possibilities for higher productivity, better workmanship and more effective management on site. It is often assumed that simple design promotes easier construction, but this is not so. Constructability can be influenced by a wide range of diverse and complex factors, and their implications both in isolation and in combination must be appreciated and understood. Even if a project is designed with constructability in mind, the

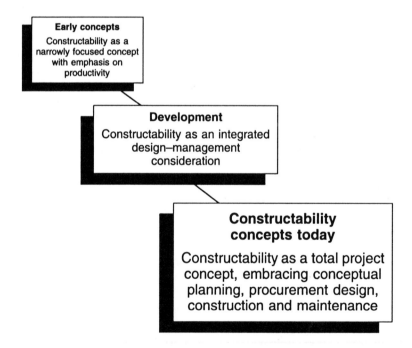

Figure 1.1   Development of constructability concepts

impact will be minimal if good intent is not complemented by accurate and effective information that translates briefing and design concepts into subsequent phases of the construction process. Communication is therefore, paramount to optimising constructability and project success.

Pioneering work in a number of countries worldwide has directed attention to the potential of constructability. Some government departments, professional institutions, influential clients, consultants and contractors in a wide range of construction industry sectors have begun to address more effectively the difficulties and problems of actively 'managing' the interface between construction phases in addition to managing the phases themselves. Historically concern may have been somewhat narrowly focused on the individual aspects of each project such as planning, resource scheduling, design rationalisation or quality control systems; today, however, the accent is upon project constructability throughout the life cycle of the building, structure or engineering works, from the conceptual planning stage to its operation, use, maintenance and perhaps even disposal. Constructability, particularly from the client's viewpoint, has become a total concept applicable to the whole of every construction project.

1.2   Development of concepts of constructability

Background: the design and construction interrelationship

There can be little doubt that over the years the construction industry has developed a unique system of interrelationships between the contractual parties. Until the advent of non-traditional forms of procurement, designers had little direct communication with the contractor in terms that truly related to how the works would be constructed, i.e. to concepts of constructability. Most communication, documentation and specifications were primarily in terms of finished work, its appearance and function. The construction industry is renowned for its lack of integration between design and construction.

Traditional procurement, although advantageous in the right circumstances, also tends inherently to exacerbate the problems of constructability. Most contractors, although sensitive to the potential of constructability, simply do not have an opportunity to promote their contribution within the procurement process, because at the tendering stage it is often too late, because it may be commercially uncompetitive to consider constructability at all, or because the client may be oblivious to the detailed analysis of value for money, mistakenly looking for it only in the consultant's presented design; as a result, constructability simply has little or no chance of reaching its full potential.

Problems, do not simply stop at procurement, of course. A lack of concern for constructability at the briefing and design stage may have knock-on effects. It is well recognised that many difficulties seen within the construction phase, and faults and defects occurring during occupation, could in many cases have been avoided had the client been in a position to have encouraged better constructability from the outset.

Recognition of the problems

Recognition of the many problems facing building and engineering practice is not new. Considerable concern has been expressed in a number of countries, and research has effectively pioneered concepts of constructability, albeit with different orientations, to address some of the difficulties.

Early experience

The Emmerson Report[2] of 1962 expressed concern at the division between the processes of design and construction, and drew attention to the lack of communication and co-ordination between the respective members of the design and construction teams. Emmerson identified a number of general problems, which still prevail to some extent, as contributing factors to potential inefficiency throughout the construction industry. The main ones were:

- inadequate preparation of design drawings and specifications before contracts are put out to tender;
- pre-contract design procedures that are inefficient owing to their complexity;
- lack of communication between architect and contractor, subcontractors and consultants.

Developing the thoughts of Emmerson, the Banwell Report[3] of 1964 suggested that:

> design and construction must be considered together and that in the traditional contracting situation, the contractor is too far removed from the design stage at which his specialised knowledge and techniques could be put to invaluable use, . . . the builder is a member of the team and should be in it from the start.

Banwell also called for greater attention to pre-contract planning and design formulation, and in particular to defining the user's requirements. Professionalism was criticised for being too narrow, and hence giving rise to unnecessary and inefficient construction practices. The Report highlighted the following needs:

- The client must define his genuine requirements clearly at the start of the formulation of the design.

- The complexities of modern construction, and its requirment for specialised techniques, demand that the design process and the construction
  phase should not be regarded as separate fields of activity.
- There should be a review of traditional contractual practices and of the
  roles of the professional parties and their codes of conduct in order to
  improve interdisciplinary relationships.

The Economic Development Council[4] in 1967 reported that the recommendations made in the Banwell Report had not been widely implemented
within the industry. Although the professions were willing to consider the use
of non-traditional contractual procedures, there was considerable reluctance
to involve the contractor in design. Flexibility in approach was advocated,
rather than radical change.

The problem of communication

Emphasising the apparent problems of communication and lack of co-ordination between contractual parties, the National Joint Consultative Committee
(NJCC) had earlier commissioned the Tavistock Institute of Human Relations to
undertake a preliminary study.[5] The findings of this study, published in
1963, identified and presented numerous examples of miscommunication
between the contractual parties. This was attributed mainly to the pattern of
relationships and the division of responsibility within the building team. It was
stated that 'effective achievement of the common design task requires full
and continuous interchange of information . . . there is a need for more
"carry-over" in the coordination function with respect to design and construction phases'. Two propositions were suggested for improving communication:

- A co-ordinating function exercised over both design and construction
  functions by a single person or single group is better than one where
  functions have different co-ordinators.
- If design and construction functions must have separate co-ordinators
  then the best system of this kind is one where there is an early exchange
  of relevant information.

The need for collaboration

In 1967, in an article in *Construction Technology*,[6] Smith stated that 'Collaboration is essential if satisfactory results are to be achieved . . . modern
construction requires a wider variety of skills instilling the need for greater
co-operation and closer co-ordination of the people and processes involved'.
    Smith noted that on most occasions the contractor met completion dates,
but that these dates were generally unrealistic in the first place. He said that

realistic dates could be specified through closer liaison between the owner, architect, surveyor and contractor. A more collaborative and cohesive team approach was advocated, although it was well recognised that this would not occur without the firm commitment of construction professionals.

Nasmith at the same time[7] cited professional demarcation as the fundamental barrier to collaboration, commenting that the professions view collaboration as 'a sort of take-over bid by other professions', where professional rivalry does little to integrate the separate contributions. Such an attitude can be attributed to the nature of the construction process itself; as Cowan simultaneously[8] pointed out: 'In practice the engineer and consultant will stand divided in the same way as architect and contractor and the division will become more marked as each, albeit blamelessly, produces problems which the other must solve.'

The traditional building process separates design from construction through the professionalisation demanded by a contractual form. It can create an environment in which the parties defend and uphold their respective rights, and perhaps concentrate upon apportioning blame for potential deficiencies, rather than encouraging the necessary teamwork.

Improvement – but the problems still exist

The Wood Report in 1975,[9] recognised some improvement in the design–construction interrelationship within the decade following the Banwell Report. It stated that:

> The traditional separation between design and construction was found to have diminished with consequent advantages all round . . . contractors have much to offer at the design stage, especially by way of advice on contractual implications of design solutions and decisions . . . yet, methods of procurement are still such that they are brought in too late for their advice and experience to be of practical use . . . the original problems still exist.

Redefining the problem – the concept of buildability

Following the reports of Emmerson, Banwell and NEDO, the Construction Industry Research and Information Association (CIRIA) embarked upon a major programme to investigate what they regarded as the main problems of construction practice. Interest concentrated on a concept referred to as 'buildability', suggesting that construction designs were not providing value for money in terms of the efficiency with which the building process was being executed. The principal aim of the programme was to promote awareness among designers of those significant aspects of design that would enable the contractor to better give the client better value for money.

The programme report *Buildability: An Assessment,*[10] which appeared in 1983, defined buildability as 'the extent to which the design of a building facilitates ease of construction, subject to the overall requirements for the completed building'. The author's understanding of the term had two important implications:

- Buildability is not a static concept, but exists on a scale from very good to very bad. *Good* buildability demands that the design of a building, structure or other construction project inherently considers the construction (production) phase, with emphasis on the method of construction, the sequence of work, the overlap and interrelation of activities and the way in which these are incorporated into the overall design concept. Conversely, *poor* buildability signifies potential discord between the design and the construction process.
- Construction has overall requirements that may necessitate the acceptance of less than good buildability. The practicalities of construction are such that buildability cannot be the sole aim. Buildability must be weighed with other determining criteria such as time, cost and quality.

Guidelines for good buildability

Through investigation within the industry, CIRIA identified seven categories of buildability principles. While they stated that a methodological approach provided data that 'were too limited to be certain that the categories identified were final and universal', they had enough confidence to publish the seven categories as provisional guidelines, which can be summarised as follows:

- Carry out thorough investigation and design.
- Plan for essential site production requirements.
- Plan for a practical sequence of operations and early enclosure.
- Plan for simplicity of assembly and logical trade sequences.
- Detail for maximum repetition and standardisation.
- Detail for achievable tolerances.
- Specify robust and suitable materials.

Further research commissioned by CIRIA, reported by Adams in 1989,[11] developed the above seven tentative principles into sixteen more definite ones, each defined and described with the aid of practical examples. The reader should obtain a copy of Adam's book and study those in the original; meanwhile they may be briefly stated as follows:

- Investigate thoroughly.
- Consider access at the design stage.
- Consider storage at the design stage.
- Design for minimum time below ground.
- Design for early enclosure.
- Use suitable materials.
- Design for the skills available.
- Design for simple assembly.
- Plan for maximum repetition and/or standardisation.
- Maximise the use of plant.
- Allow for sensible tolerances.
- Allow for a practical sequence of operations.
- Avoid return visits by trades.
- Plan to avoid change to work by subsequent operations.
- Design for safe construction.
- Communicate clearly.

CIRIA's original report concluded with two important points, namely:

- When good buildability has been adequately defined and developed, it leads to major benefits for clients, designers and contractors.
- The achievement of good buildability depends upon both designers and contractors being able to see the whole construction process through each others' eyes.

Thus the early work of CIRIA focused upon the potential of the design process to influence buildability, and their later work, presented by Adams, widened the scope a little, developing a greater number of basic principles that pointed towards the multi-faceted nature of buildability. The efforts of CIRIA, and others have laid some groundwork that allows the problems of the construction industry to be better understood, and have also pointed to broader fields of study. It is this more general consideration of the ideas involved that has focused attention on the concept of constructability.

Further significant studies

A number of studies[12, 13] have addressed, in some way, the disparity between design and construction; these highlight the following requirements: the early involvement of the contractor in the procurement process, the overlapping of design and construction functions using 'fast-tracking' techniques, and, more radically, the adoption of non-traditional contractual approaches. Of these studies, the National Economic Development Council Report, *Faster Building for Industry*,[14] presents the principal problems and identifies the need for bridging the divide between design and construction. These are summarised as follows:

- The general belief that speed costs money is quite unfounded, fast construction is possible without penalty to either cost or quality. Responsibilities within the team must be clearly defined and, in particular, the client must know who is the team leader.
- Organisation of the contractor under traditional procurement procedures can create unnecessary complexity for the client.
- Traditional methods of design and tendering can give good results; however, on average, non-traditional techniques tend to be quicker. Within the traditional approach, both tendering on bills of approximate quantities and choosing the contractor through a negotiated tender lead to faster progress.
- Preparation of the design must be directed toward facilitating progress on site.
- The design must take account of buildability, allowing the procurement of materials and the performance of the different building operations to be planned and organised as straightforwardly as possible, so as to result in a minimum of disruption.
- Contributions from specialist consultants, the contractor, subcontractors and suppliers must be obtained within sufficient time for their effective co-ordination and input into the design function.
- Contractors should not be selected on the basis of price alone; their ability should be assessed also. Early recruitment of the contractor, before the design is finalised, may assist in the anticipation of site problems and produce a more economic and more buildable design.
- Efficient progress on site requires effective site management, clear communication between the client, architect and contractor and detailed feedback mechanisms to control progress.
- It is not the form of contract that is the determining factor in meeting the requirements of the construction process; it is the attitudes of the parties. The standard forms of contract invoke penalties for delays and no incentives for efficiency. The industry must look for ways of sharing the benefits accrued from improved performance.

Constructability in the United States

The decline in the cost-effectiveness and quality of the American construction industry in the late 1970s stimulated the industry's clients in the form of the Business Roundtable to establish the Construction Industry Cost Effectiveness Project study team. Their report concludes that the benefits to be gained from 'good' constructability are approximately ten to twenty times the cost of achieving it. Its recommendations include:

- that training materials and reference manuals be developed on constructability;

- that constructability practice should be included as part of tertiary education;
- that project owners should become more aware of methods and benefits of constructability.

These findings stimulated the establishment of the Construction Industry Institute (CII) in 1983, with a mission to improve the cost effectiveness, total quality management and international competitiveness of the construction industry. Based in the University of Texas at Austin, it is a partnership of owners, contractors and academia. Constructability has been a major aim of the CII, with a number of studies undertaken by the constructability task force which has developed into an implementation task force that examines means to aid penetration into the industry's practices.

The CII definition of constructability is 'the optimum integration of construction knowledge and experience in planning, engineering, procurement and field operations to achieve overall project objectives'.[15] This emphasises both the ability to construct and the importance of construction input into all project phases.

Research by the CII task force had a number of stages. First, Tatum et al.[16] focused on three areas that it was felt could improve constructability during conceptual planning:

- development of the project plan;
- laying out of the site;
- selection of major construction methods.

Their work was based on fifteen case studies in industrial, commercial and public infrastructure buildings.

The second study by O'Connor et al.[17] looked at how construction knowledge could be most effectively utilised during the engineering and procurement phases of a project. It derived seven concepts:

- Design and procurement schedules are construction-driven.
- Designs are configured to enable efficient construction.
- Design elements are standardised and repetition is taken advantage of.
- Pre-assembly work is scoped in advance and module and/or pre-assembly designs are prepared to facilitate fabrication, transport and installation.
- Designs promote the accessibility of manpower, material and equipment.
- Designs facilitate construction under adverse weather conditions when they exist.
- Specifications are reviewed in detail by owner, designer and construction personnel and serve to simplify the field construction process.

The third study, by O'Connor and Davis,[18] researched the constructability improvements that can be made during field operations. The bulk of the data were obtained through site interviews on fourteen projects, with an average cost of US$348 million and a duration of twenty-six months. The study identified seven issues that may involve innovative construction, which relate to the following:

- sequencing of field tasks;
- temporary construction materials and/or system;
- hand tools;
- construction equipment;
- constructor optional pre-assembly;
- temporary facilities directly supportive of field methods;
- post-bid construction preferences.

The CII in Texas integrated the three studies into a single 'constructability concepts file,'[19] which has six concepts defined for the conceptual planning phase, seven concepts defined for the design and procurement phases and one concept for the field operations phase. The purpose of the concepts file is to stimulate thinking; it is not intended to be a checklist, which it was thought would run the risk of being too prescriptive. This approach recognises the uniqueness of each project in the construction industry and the risks in applying a checklist indiscriminately without proper attention to the individual nature of any project.

The importance of the CII work is the promotion of a total constructability system (Fig. 1.2) of which the Concepts File is a part, but which places emphasis on the commitment and adoption of the programme.[20] The essence of the system is an understanding of the cost–influence curve, leading to the implementation of the programme, which has seven components:

- *Self assessment*   The extent to which the organisation achieves constructability.
- *Policy*   A written policy towards constructability.
- *Executive sponsor*   A senior executive with commitment to the implementation of constructability.
- *Organisation*   An organisation that promotes adoption of constructability.
- *Procedure*   How to implement constructability – through the concepts file.
- *Appraisal*   Review of success, lessons learned.
- *Database*   Logging of constructability savings for later reference.

Companies in the United States are now adopting the CII's constructability concepts. At the CII's annual conference in 1989 the president of Dow

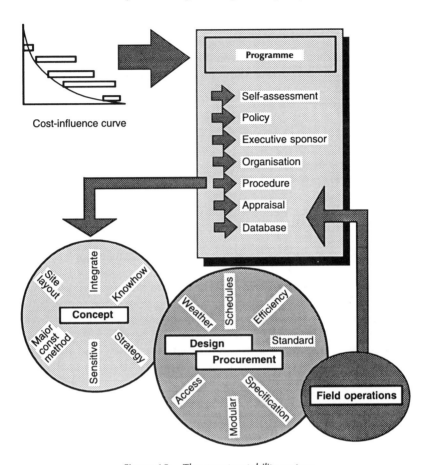

Figure 1.2   The constructability system

Chemicals reported that his company had tested out constructability on three multimillion-dollar projects, achieving a 5 per cent saving on cost and a 13 per cent saving on time. Some organisations such as the Houston Business Roundtable, Kelloggs, Brown Root Brown, and Chevron have each developed their own, more detailed constructability concepts file.

The CII implementation task force recognises the dilemma between a concepts file that resists specificity and the general need expressed by individual organisations for more particular tools and techniques. The task force also explored the notion of tying constructability concepts more directly to the various stages in the project life cycle, the idea being that if users can follow the project life cycle stage by stage with a checklist of concepts to apply at each stage then such a 'road map' may direct them to appropriate concepts as they progress through the project.

The American Society of Civil Engineers (ASCE)[21] in 1974 reported on practices defining and examining what they considered to be the important tasks of a professional construction manager, finding the provision of 'constructability' to be one of the most prominent of these. The ASCE study suggested six major considerations to provide the best practical recipe for constructability, which may be summarised as follows:

- Evaluating various design configurations to optimise owner requirements;
- knowing the various project systems and their interface requirements with other project components;
- understanding trade skills and practices, construction methods, materials, labour and subcontract resources and plant and equipment;
- appreciating local and climatic conditions;
- evaluating site conditions, both above and below ground, and realising their possible implications upon construction;
- determining availability of space and access routes on site.

Further research[1] investigating construction resourcing and management has assigned particular responsibilities to construction management for the express purpose of improving project constructability. These are summarised as follows:

- participation in conceptual development and planning for the project;
- participation in decision making;
- participation in design review, scheduling and cost estimating;
- being available for consultation in construction-related problems;
- ensuring construction management input in the design phase.

It can be seen quite clearly from the above that while early practice had in the main focused on the design element, in later studies the accent has tended to be on examining the role of the contractor or the construction management function.

1.3   Development of the principles of constructability

Constructability in Australia

In the overheated economy of the 1980s, Australia's construction industry was criticised for its poor performance and service to its clients. The New South Wales government established a Royal Commission into the building industry led by Roger Gyles QC,[22] and its findings included evidence of collusive tendering practices by contractors and industrial anarchy and intimidation by unions, as well as cost and time overruns in the order of 28 per cent. Crane drivers in Sydney were earning up to A$150 000 per year when their award wage was supposed to be more like A$40 000.

Some of the research and case studies contributing to the Commission's findings were undertaken by Ireland who has undertaken a number of studies of management and efficiency in construction. In an analysis of the performance of twenty-five high rise projects in Sydney[23, 24] he found two of the most significant variables to be the extent of 'construction planning during design' and 'managerial actions'. Later work[25, 26] extended to comparison of Australian management practices with those in the United States and United Kingdom. He found that the time spent on buildability analysis during design in Australia averaged approximately two person-years on an office building, compared with only four person-months in the United States. Ireland's studies have also shown that Australian projects, in terms of actual days worked, are constructed at the same rate as, or slightly faster than, those in the United States or United Kingdom. However, in overall terms construction is slower owing to time lost because of industrial disputes, inclement weather and public holidays.

During that period it was common for industrial disputation to add around 10 per cent to construction time and down time due to inclement weather a further 10 per cent, while Ireland's comparison cites typical US construction projects as having 19 days' holidays, whereas Australian projects have up to 41 days off for vacation, public holidays and rostered days.

In a perverse way, the difficult industrial relations environment in the Australian construction industry has forced contractors to think through the construction implications of design in advance, which has very often resulted in more constructable solutions; examples include the following:

- reduction of the number of different trades involved in components, reducing the likelihood of demarcation disputes;
- prefabrication off site, reducing the risk of on-site disputation and separating job site boundaries;
- early achievement of weather tightness;
- segregation of job sites, rationalising construction types and containing unions' spheres of influence.

Research at the University of Melbourne by Hon, Gairns and Wilson[27] investigated a number of case studies in a project management setting; these authors concluded that:

- The contribution of construction personnel to the design of the projects studied was significant.

- The iterative relationship between construction and design led to tangible benefits.
- Rationalisation of design, which involves simplification, modularisation and repetition of design detailing, is essential to the achievement of buildability.
- The achievement of buildability is influenced by technical factors (building technology and/or systems, project planning and scheduling, etc.) in the building process.
- There are many other factors, particularly non-technical factors associated with the management of building projects, which need to be considered as part of the process of achieving buildability.

These technical and non-technical factors affecting constructability, identified by Hon,[28] have been expressed diagrammatically by Francis,[29] as shown in Figure 1.3.

McGeorge, Chen and Ostwald[30] challenged the traditional view of constructability as being primarily concerned with the design and construction phases of a project, and proposed that constructability must encompass the life cycle of a building. The completion of a building for handover should be seen not as an end-point in time but as part of a continuum. The impact of decisions to reduce construction times may in fact adversely affect the use or maintenance of the building in the future. Therefore constructability does not equate simply to the ease of construction, but is also concerned with the appropriateness of the finished project. These authors' definition of constructability is 'the extent to which decisions made during the whole building procurement process, in response to factors influencing the project and other project goals, ultimately facilitate the ease of construction and the quality of the completed project'.

McGeorge *et al.* propose a three-dimensional conceptual model, the dimensions being the participants (stakeholders and decision makers), the constructability factors (exogenous factors, endogenous factors or project goals) and the stages of the building procurement process (from feasibility to post-occupation). They believe that greater gains are likely to be made in terms of the management of the building procurement process than in construction technology. It is not lack of information that affects constructability, but rather the lack of management information. They propose the development of a constructability index or scale based on indicators for success, rather than concentrating on what went wrong with projects.

In response to the key issues identified by the New South Wales Royal Commission into Productivity in the Building Industry, namely

- industrial relations,
- best practice and
- anti-fraud measures,

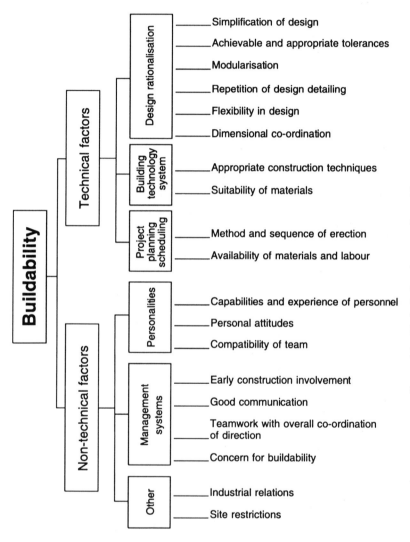

Figure 1.3   Technical and non-technical factors

the NSW government public sector promulgated a *Capital Project Procurement Manual* (CPPM)[31] as a basis for the reform of the Industry. The NSW government has consolidated its purchasing power, so that all sectors follow the guidelines of the CPPM. Their buildability policy adopts McGeorge's definition and sets out a series of principles and issues:

- Site factors:
    - physical features;
    - access and egress;
    - geotechnical;
    - material availability;
    - workforce and/or skill availability;
    - weather;
    - workspace.
- Design:
    - details;
    - time cost and quality requirements;
    - maintenance;
    - operational requirements;
    - material selection;
    - structure type;
    - workplace reform;
    - layout flexibility;
    - services location and/or requirements;
    - complexity.
- Constructability:
    - site area;
    - type of site;
    - site access and egress;
    - extent of site work on and off;
    - mix of materials;
    - programming requirements;
    - time to achieve weather proofing.
- Employee relations:
    - number, mix and sequencing of trades;
    - industrial relations;
    - enterprise agreements;
    - contractor past performance with employee relations;
    - promotion of multi-skilling.
- Safety:
    - code requirements;
    - reduction of work at heights;
    - inclusion of safety features;
    - safety in maintenance works.

- Climatic conditions:
  - design inclusions;
  - securing protected work areas;
  - dry access to site amenities;
  - service penetrations;
  - access within the site.
- Procurement methods:
  - management of the procurement process;
  - selection of a procurement system;
  - delivery systems;
  - contract systems;
  - risk analysis.

The CPPM includes advice on implementation, advocating a team approach that engenders responsibility from each participant in order to achieve the most effective result for the client. A critical element in the implementation of constructability for public-sector projects is the prescriptive nature of publicly accountable procurement systems. CPPM addresses this issue both for construct-only or design-development-and-construct contracts by nominating the client's project manager as responsible for implementing the buildability assessment. For such contracts, direct action will be required to ensure that construction expertise is input into the earliest feasibility stage and then throughout the design process. The means to obtain such expertise may include:

- the use of the government's in-house construction team, or
- the acquisition of industry expertise either via specialist consultants or by the employment of industry contractors.

The CPPM rounds off its policy on buildability with an action plan designed to assist in ensuring that all issues are addressed at particular stages in the project program.

Construction Industry Institute, Australia

In 1991–3 the Construction Industry Institute, Australia (CIIA) collaborated with the CII in the United States to develop a constructability principles file appropriate for the Australian context.[32] A task force was established at the University of South Australia. The researchers visited the United States and the United Kingdom to evaluate the latest developments and to learn from the experiences of practitioners and researchers. Companies in the United States were able to provide hard evidence of actual savings.

The set of principles developed, which consists of a system for improving the level of constructability achieved on a project, is dependent on the client being committed to its inclusion in the project procedures from the start. It involves the whole project team, from the very beginning of the project, considering the effects of their actions on the construction process. The main contractor should be included in the project team from the feasibility stage onwards.

The research team evaluated the overseas concepts against a series of local case studies and developed a set of principles tailored to the Australian industry. These were evaluated and tested and some twenty case examples included in the research database.

The system developed for Australia consists of a best-practice, how-to-do-it manual with the following contents:

1. Implementation advice on how organisations can establish a constructability program.
2. Flowchart indicating the applicability of the principles of constructability at the various stages of the project life cycle.
3. Executive summaries of the principles of constructability.
4. Twelve principles of constructability.
5. Database to record examples of savings from constructability.

The implementation section is expressed in general terms to account for the individual cultures of many organisations. Key issues for successful implementation are covered, rather than providing specific procedures which may not suit all organisations and therefore reduce the likelihood of their continued use.

An important development by the South Australian task force is the concept that principles of constructability are not applied sequentially as the building process develops, but may be applied at a variety of stages. The task force developed a flowchart or roadmap (Figure 1.4), which advises the user which principles are most likely to be relevant at particular stages in the project life cycle.

The principles file comprises twelve overriding concepts of constructability. They represent current best practice in constructability and are aimed at encouraging the project team to apply them, where appropriate, to their projects. While the team may find some principles directly applicable to their particular project, the goal of the file is to stimulate thought about constructability and how to make it work. The system avoids a 'checklist' approach that stifles creative thought, and addresses the difficulties associated with implementation by indicating the relative importance of each principle at any particular stage of a 'typical' project. The twelve principles are given in Figure 1.5.

The database contains examples of savings from constructability on some Australian projects. These are intended as samples only, and it is anticipated that individual companies will use the database to record their own experiences. In this way constructability can be improved in projects in the future, as lessons learned are recalled and reused where appropriate.

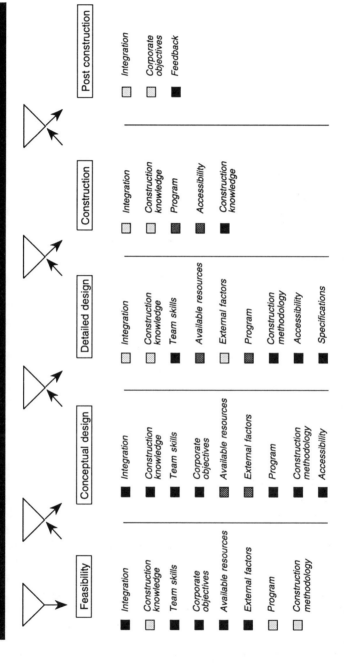

Figure 1.4   Constructability flowchart (CII, Australia)

Principles of Constructability

1. **Integration**
   Constructability must be made an integral part of the project plan.

2. **Construction knowledge**
   Project planning must actively involve construction knowledge and experience.

3. **Team skills**
   The experience, skills and composition of the project team must be appropriate for the project.

4. **Corporate objectives**
   Constructability is enhanced when the project team gains an understanding of the client's corporate and project objectives.

5. **Available resources**
   The technology of the design solution must be matched with the skills and resources available.

6. **External factors**
   External factors can affect the cost and/or program of the project.

7. **Program**
   The overall program for the project must be realistic and construction-sensitive, and have the commitment of the project team.

8. **Construction methodology**
   The project design must consider construction methodology.

9. **Accessiblity**
   Constructability will be enhanced if construction accessibility is considered in the design and construction stages of the project.

10. **Specifications**

    Project constructability is enhanced when construction efficiency is considered in specification development.

11. **Construction innovation**
    The use of innovative techniques during construction will enhance constructability.

12. **Feedback**
    Constructability can be enhanced on similar future projects if a post-construction analysis is undertaken by the project team.

Figure 1.5   Constructability principles (CII, Australia)

Application of the principles

The first three principles, INTEGRATION, CONSTRUCTION KNOWLEDGE and TEAM SKILLS, address the importance of making constructability part of normal project procedures and involving the 'right people' from the very beginning of the project. The next principle, CORPORATE OBJECTIVES, looks at how constructability can be enhanced when the project team understands the corporate objectives, as well as the project ones. AVAILABLE RESOURCES and EXTERNAL FACTORS address the fact that constructability will often be affected by factors over which the project team has little control, but whose influence can be minimised if identified early.

The principle entitled PROGRAM outlines the importance of having a realistic, construction-sensitive program that has been developed and agreed by the whole project team. CONSTRUCTION METHODOLOGY, ACCESSIBILITY and SPECIFICATIONS relate to issues that need to be integrated into the final design and documentation of the project.

The eleventh principle, CONSTRUCTION INNOVATION, addresses the use of construction knowledge to improve the effectiveness of operations on site. Where constructability is correctly integrated into a project, the best solution has already been identified, evaluated and documented, with the constructor's assistance, prior to tender. Therefore, although the ability to influence cost during construction is less significant than in the feasibility or design stages, *collectively* savings from constructability made during this time can be substantial.

The final principle, FEEDBACK, relates to the concept of the life cycle of a project being a cyclical, cumulative process rather than a linear one, whereby information can be used in similar projects in the future. Two post-construction reviews are recommended; these are especially concerned with evaluating the effect of decisions regarding constructability on construction efficiency and the operational efficiency of the project.

1.4   Constructability: stages of consideration

In reviewing empirical practices surrounding and developing the general concept of constructability, it can be seen quite clearly that attention is gradually being redirected towards examining its multidimensional aspect rather than merely focusing upon isolated issues within design or production. Once this is appreciated, it is quite natural to view constructability in its true context as a managerial system embracing all aspects of the total building or engineering processes. It is also true to say that constructability today has developed into a concept that is becoming more client-led. Many of its ideas depend upon the client insisting on its inclusion in project formulation and development. As the general perception and stance of construction clients has changed over recent years, so too has constructability from the early narrow focus on buildability to the multidimensional total process concept.

Constructability is therefore:

a system for achieving optimum integration of construction knowledge in the building process and balancing the various project and environmental constraints to achieve maximisation of project goals and building performance (CII, Australia)

(See Figure 1.6.)

Constructability must be considered from the first notional idea suggested by the client, and is quite simply a prerequisite throughout what may be considered to be a staged process (see Figure 1.7). It is essential to consider constructability at an early stage in the total construction process, because the ability to influence project cost, and so value for money, from the client's viewpoint, diminishes as the project progresses in time. During the stages listed below, constructability consideration should focus on the items listed for each stage:

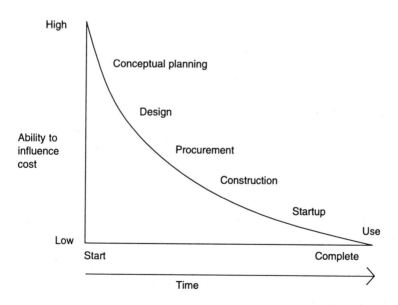

Figure 1.6   Constructability cost-influence curve (CII, USA)

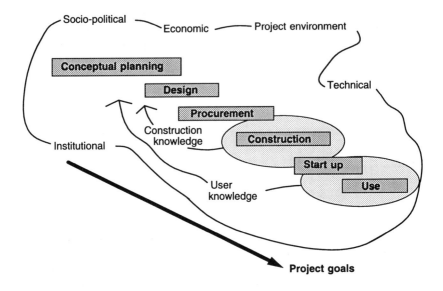

Figure 1.7   The wider framework of the influence of constructability

'Constructability is a system for achieving optimum integration of construction knowledge in the building process and balancing the various project and environmental constraints to achieve maximisation of project goals and building performance' (CII, Australia).

- *Conceptual planning and briefing*   Corporate objectives; integration; available resources; team skills; external factors.
- *Design*:   Team skills; construction methodology; accessibility; specifications.
- *Procurement*   Corporate objectives; overall programme; integration; team skills.
- *Construction (production)*   Construction knowledge; site programme; innovation; accessibility; the most efficient use of resources.
- *Post-construction (startup and use)*   Feedback.

Constructability is the propensity of all aspects of a building or engineering project to enable optimum utilisation of construction resources. Good constructability may improve design empathy for production, encourage more effective communication between the parties, simplify construction techniques and optimise construction management approach. Poor constructability may, conversely, fail to achieve these objectives. Implementation is not always straightforward, and may not always be possible; also, realistically, constructability is simply not achievable without some cost.

Constructability must also take account of the problems that do exist, and the practical trade-off between the objectives possible and the real cost of achieving these objectives. In an ideal world, constructability would be a concept for application *per se* but unfortunately the real world simply precludes this. Implications for time, cost and quality must be realised and assessed, and strategies and approaches for achieving benefits both desirable and practical must be evolved and implemented.

1.5   Benefits of good constructability

Modern construction clients expect their projects to be completed on time, within the anticipated budget, and to be of good quality; that is, they demand inherently a high quality of service and value for money. The benefits are clearly seen in the end-product and this should be justification alone for a client to encourage constructability. Moreover, clients also expect the product to be trouble-free and relatively inexpensive to use and maintain. They expect a whole package, and rely for this upon good constructability. This should also serve to stimulate the designer into pursuing constructability. He is seeking to simplify design, reduce drawing office cost and make easier his management role on-site. Although it may take more time to produce more constructable design solutions rather than stock solutions, this drawback should be outweighed by advantages later in the process. Poor constructability simply means trouble for the client and designer later on, because time saved in the design process by the reduced or inappropriate consideration of constructability is only likely to be lost again during the construction phase.

Constructability means benefit to the contractor also, since consideration of the work at the design stage and prior to and during construction should make work more systematic, better co-ordinated and more efficient. There will be increased demands on supervision, but again this must be balanced against the cost of not providing adequate supervision. The knock-on effects of poor constructability are the longer-term problems of user difficulty and inappropriate maintenance and repair, which can, obviously, hold implications for later design and construction. This again, alone, is justification, one would think, for taking constructability seriously. Conversely, there is little doubt that good constructability can enhance the designer's and contractor's reputation, minimise the waste of resources and produce a finished product with better quality and fewer defects. These factors make further compelling arguments for constructability.

There are many all-round benefits of good constructability; these are measurable not only in cost and time, but also in terms of the physiological and psychological gains for the participants in the total construction process; they include:

- more effective procurement;
- better design;
- more effective planning;
- improved site management;
- increased project performance;
- efficient management of problems;
- improved quality;
- fewer delays and disruptions;
- lower cost of remedial and repeat works;
- provision of feedback for future projects;
- enhanced recognition for participants;
- increased job satisfaction;
- better communications;
- less acrimonious interrelationships;
- increased co-operation and discussion;
- greater empathy for the contribution of others.

These are benefits that stretch right across the total construction process and all are achievable through good constructability practices.

1.6   Barriers to implementation

Creating a building, structure or engineering works that is easier to construct or assemble should not be regarded as the sole aim of constructability. Consideration of constructability is not sacrosanct to a designer or a contractor *per se*, since construction professionals are employed by a client and the client's brief will present an array of demands to satisfy – user requirements, time frame, cost budget, and workmanship levels to name but a few.

Construction projects do not materialise on a production line; rather, each evolves individually and is usually unique. Designers and contractors use different approaches to reach the same end. Such differences, of course, give variety and novelty and provide the vital ingredient of competitiveness. Constructability invites the consideration of a multitude of fundamental aspects and variables, including: site conditions; sequence of operations; utilisation of resources; specification of materials. The manipulation of such aspects, together with the requirements for speed of construction and keeping within the budgeted cost, means that constructability must be encouraged so as to achieve the benefits available but not detract from the finished product.

It is clear that good constructability can only evolve from the integration of the contractual parties and a concentrated effort towards project teamwork. Improvement in constructability in design approach, construction techniques and managerial arrangements will result directly from better project integration, but it is also clear that such benefit will result from personal effort and innovation by the contributors. In addition, market forces and the need to be competitive should influence better constructability. These macro level advantages will result directly from clients who are seeking better ways to administer their projects.

If the payoff from constructability is so characteristic, why are its principles not known more widely and used more readily? Constructability concepts are undoubtedly hindered by what can only be described as *barriers to implementation*. The most prominent of these are:

- *Client resistance*   There is considerable resistance on the part of many clients who, through a lack of knowledge and understanding, do not realise the benefits that may accrue from constructability. In addition, the conscious pursuit of constructability will add extra and visible cost to a project, and if the client is unable to believe in the benefits then he will inevitably shy away from it.
- *Traditional building process*   Tradition is perhaps the biggest single cause of resistance to the wider use of concepts of constructability. In the traditional building process the contractual parties, in particular the designer and the contractor, are formally separated by the very terms of the contract. Standard forms of contract invariably establish the rights and responsibilities of the parties within a framework that prepares for possible adversarial outcomes. Traditional selective tendering procedures further exacerbate this situation, and one may even cite tradition as the bugbear of training and education within the industry, particularly when each construction discipline is effectively regarded as an isolated profession.
- *Professional demarcation*   Construction professionals are generally unaccustomed to close integration or working outside their traditional professional parameters; nor are contractors generally encouraged to contribute to their full potential at the earliest stage in the construction process, again because of professional demarcation.
- *Project priorities*   Because clients may be unaware of the real potential of constructability, and more ready to accept the status quo, project priorities tend to be cost- and time-oriented, with integration of the project phases and participants a lower priority.
- *Incentives*   Given the continual, widespread use of traditional procurement, standard forms of contract and traditional tendering there is little incentive for the parties to integrate or operate outside their usual remit.
- *Education*   The normal training and education patterns of the professions are established on a discipline basis, with a strong tendency to develop individualism within each of the disciplines and separation between them. Architects, engineers, and construction managers have always been educated separately in the main, although today there are

some signs of progress away from this, through integrated faculties and schools of construction and the built environment, together with integrated postgraduate studies.

- *Qualified personnel*   Given some of the aspects identified, it is generally difficult to obtain personnel who have the intrinsic capability, skills and desire to improve potential constructability in the projects they work on. In-house training will obviously help here, but only as a product of the individual employer's concerns and aspirations.

It is obvious that the segregated nature of construction and the particular characteristics of contractual arrangements will create inherent barriers to the pursuit of constructability. More fundamental than this, however, are the primary obstacles to general advancement and innovation within design, construction technology and management that are brought about by the fragmentation of the construction industry, the highly competitive stance that must be assumed by the individual participants and the attitude of some within the industry who do not contemplate change or cannot readily embrace it. These difficulties and barriers exist, are complex and involved and will not be overcome simply.

1.7   The search for better constructability

We have seen that a considerable awareness exists of the potential improvements that constructability can bring and equally that there is wide appreciation of the problems and difficulties in implementing it. The benefits of good constructability, and the consequences of poor constructability, are perhaps best appreciated by construction professionals themselves. Methods must be developed that formalise the professionals' understanding of constructability in such a way as to achieve a wider, more genuine knowledge of the concepts involved. There need to be greater awareness and understanding across the construction professions: an established constructability empathy.

There is little doubt that good constructability can result in tangible financial benefits for the client. It is also clear that it can lead to more straightforward design and lower development costs for the designer, and produce simpler construction and lower production costs for the contractor. What is not so well appreciated is the potential benefits that exist when constructability is taken into account in the fields of procurement options, life cycle of product use, and maintenance of the final product.

Traditional procurement has tended, in many cases, to marginalise the potential of constructability. One approach to achieving better constructability may be to use a contractual procedure in which the contractor plays a part in project formulation earlier in the project evolutionary cycle – as in non-traditional design-build, for example; such an approach works in theory, and is also known to work in practice, but is, in some cases it just differs too radically from established practice, and can of course tie the client to a particular system that may be ill-suited to his overall requirements. Therefore, ways have to be found to establish guidelines, principles and rules for constructability that are simple enough to understand, are acceptable to all and actually make a definite contribution to the construction process. If more general principles and procedures are suggested then it will enable the participants in the project to distinguish facets of good and bad constructability throughout so that by means of integrated teamwork and collaboration the financial benefits of good constructability are achieved by client, designer, contractor and user.

This leads us to defining the steps that need to be taken to succeed in such an endeavour. Certainly, empirical studies such as the pioneering work of CIRIA have identified principles of good constructability in basic technical terms. Similarly, subsequent research has laid the basis for widening the scope of understanding in the management of construction projects. What is required now is a recognised framework and a set of strategies for implementing the recognised principles and so integrating the individual contributions in order to produce better constructability across the total construction process. Constructability is about focusing clearly on client needs, optimising design input, maximising design and construction collaboration and following through the process to the use and maintenance of the finished product.

References

1. Business Roundtable, *Integrating Construction Resources and Technology into Engineering*, Business Roundtable, New York, November 1982, Report B-1.
2. H. Emmerson, *Survey of Problems Before the Construction Industry*, a report prepared for the Ministry of Works, London, 1962.
3. H. Banwell, *The Placing and Management of Contracts for Building and Civil Engineering Work*, HMSO, London, 1964.
4. Economic Development Council, *Action on the Banwell Report*, HMSO, London, 1967.
5. Tavistock Institute of Human Relations, *Communication in the Building Industry: The Report of a Pilot Study*, Tavistock Publications, London, (1963).
6. R. Smith, 'Collaboration: A Civil Engineering Contractor's Viewpoint', *Construction Technology*, (June) pp. 24–5.
7. J. D. Nasmith, 'Collaboration in Building', *Construction Technology* (June) pp. 19–21.
8. J. Cowan, 'Collaboration: As a Civil Engineer Sees It', *Construction Technology* (June), pp. 23–4.
9. National Economic Development Office (NEDO) *The Wood Report: The Public Client and the Construction Industry*, HMSO, London, 1975.
10. Construction Industry Research and Information Association (CIRIA), *Buildability: An Assessment*, CIRIA Publications, London, 1983, Special Publication no. 26.
11. S. Adams, *Practical Buildability*, CIRIA/Butterworths, London, 1989
12. A. Griffith, *Buildability: The Effect of Design and Management on Construction, A Case Study*, SERC/Heriot-Watt University, Edinburgh, 1985.

13. National Economic Development Office (NEDO), *Achieving Quality on Building Sites*, NEDO, London, 1987.
14. National Economic Development Office (NEDO), *Faster Building for Industry*, HMSO, London, 1983.
15. Construction Industry Institute (CII), *Constructability – A Primer*, Publication 3–1, CII University of Texas, Austin, July 1986.
16. C. B. Tatum, J. A. Vanegas, and J. M. Williams, *Constructability Improvement during Conceptual Planning*, CII, University of Texas, Austin, 1986.
17. J.T. O'Connor, S. E. Rusch, and M. J. Schulz, *Constructability Improvement during Engineering and Procurement*, CII, University of Texas, Austin, (1986).
18. J.T. O'Connor, and J. S. Davis, 'Constructability during Field Operations', *Journal of Construction Engineering and Management*, vol. 114, (1988), no. 4.
19. Construction Industry Institute (CII), *Constructability Concepts File*, CII, University of Texas, Austin, 1987.
20. Construction Industry Institute (CII), 'Guidelines for implementing a constructability program', CII, University of Texas, Austin, July 1987, Publication 3–2.
21. American Society of Civil Engineers (ASCE), 'Professional Construction Management Services', *Journal of Construction Services* (1974).
22. R. Gyles, *Report of the Royal Commission into the Building Industry*, Government Secretariat, NSW, Australia, (1992).
23. V. Ireland, 'The Role of Managerial Actions in the Cost, Time and Quality Performance of Commercial Building Projects', PhD Thesis, University of Sydney, unpublished, (1983).
24. V. Ireland, 'The Role of Managerial Actions in the Cost, Time and Quality Performance of High-Rise Commercial Building Projects', *Construction Management and Economics*, vol. 3, (1985).
25. V. Ireland, 'A Comparison of US, UK and Australia Management Practice with Special Reference to Lost Time', *The Building Economist*, vol. 26 (1987) no. 3.
26. V. Ireland, 'Management Efficiency and the Constructor', *The Building Economist*, vol. 27 (1988), no. 1.
27. S. L. Hon, D. A. Gairns and Wilson, O. D. 'Buildability: A Review of Research and Practice', *Australian Institute of Building Papers*, vol. 3 (1988/9).
28. S. L. Hon, 'A Study of Buildability within a Project Management System', Master of Building Thesis, University of Melbourne (1988), unpublished.
29. V. E. Francis, 'Implementation of Constructability into Australian Construction Projects', Master of Applied Science in Project Management Thesis, University of South Australia, 1994, unpublished.
30. D. McGeorge, S. E. Chen, and M. J. Ostwald, 'The Development of a Conceptual Model of Buildability which Identifies User Satisfaction as a Major Objective', Paper, CIB Conference, Rotterdam, 1992.
31. New South Wales Government Construction, Policy Steering Committee, *Capital Project Procurement Manual*, NSW, Australia, October 1993.
32. Construction Industry Institute (CII), Australia, *Constructability Principles File*, CII, University of South Australia, Adelaide, Australia, 1993.

2 Strategies for Constructability

Chapter 1 considered the interrelationship between design and construction, which is paramount to the successful consideration of constructability in modern construction projects. This was emphasised in a review of the background and evolutionary development of constructability concepts, which focused both on practice and on various research reports, some well known and some less so, that have been conducted over many years. These studies highlight some of the perceived shortcomings in the construction process and emphasise the need for greater attention to the implementation of constructability. This chapter first identifies the need for consideration of constructability and introduces the main factors of influence upon constructability which are considered in subsequent chapters. This chapter next considers the necessity for all contributors to the construction process to participate actively in the search for better constructability, that is, constructability is considered as a strategy for action throughout the total construction process.

2.1 The need for constructability

The inefficiency of the construction process

Many studies of construction practice[1–10] have reviewed the implications of inadequate design and production methods within both traditional and non-traditional construction and in a variety of types of building and engineering.

The National Economic Development Office (NEDO) report *Achieving quality on Building Sites*[11] presents the findings of a study into the standard of work achieved in general building construction. Of over five hundred examples of inadequate quality on construction sites, some two-thirds were adjudged due to design inefficiencies. It was seen that many problems were caused by unclear or missing project information, inadequacies in the quality of information provided or a lack of complete information, and/or a general lack of co-ordination of design with construction. The remaining problems were apportioned to poor workmanship by contractors and subcontractors, general management inefficiencies and/or a lack of care on site. Poor constructability was clearly a significant contributor to the difficulties which emerged.

Causes of problems, difficulties and shortcomings in construction

Most shortcomings identified in practice, such as those described, can be broadly traced to the following construction processes and causes:

1. *Procurement and design*   Problems occurring in:

- understanding client requirements;
- information in project documentation;
- consideration of regional and/or situational characteristics;
- forethought and consideration to user requirements;
- knowledge of the performance characteristics of materials and components;
- completion of design details;
- co-ordination among the phases of design;
- co-ordination between design and construction;
- consideration of modular co-ordination;
- analysis of cost in the decision-making process of design, construction and maintenance;

2. *Material and components (fabrication)*   Problems occurring in:

- standardisation of materials and components;
- modular co-ordination;
- efficiency of quality control in the fabrication process;
- productivity, (high level of wastage in manufacture);
- protection during delivery to site;
- diffusion of information about the use of the products;

3. *Construction (production)*   Problems occurring in:

- standardisation;
- perception of design requirement;
- alterations to the design specification;
- control in receiving materials on site;
- knowledge of performance characteristics of materials and components (specification);
- information for the use of new materials (innovation);
- continuity of construction operations (programme);
- acceptance of workmanship and use of quality control systems on-site;
- planning (site operations and material procurement);
- site layout;
- co-ordination of trade gangs;
- communication and recording information;
- protection of materials on site;
- level of wastage on site;
- use of management systems;
- productivity of workforce on site;
- supervision (cost and productivity);
- conditions of work (environment, health, safety, etc.);
- formal training of workforce and high turnover.

4. *Use and maintenance*   Problems occurring in:

- standardisation – insufficient documentation;
- instructions for use, operation and maintenance;
- routine and preventive maintenance;
- appreciation of the use of the building.

All of these deficiencies, frequently seen within building and engineering processes, result, in the main, from the lack of consideration for the principles of constructability.

Constructability: sensitivity to the problems

The one aspect that emerges throughout the many investigations is the general lack of co-ordination between, and control of, the design and construction phases, whether this is reflected in a design or engineering fault or in poor workmanship on site.

Leaving aside the topical argument that it is the traditional approach to contractual form that is partly or wholly responsible for the present shortcomings in the construction process, or that design-and-build contracts, package deals and variations in managerial approach are an obvious solution to the problems that beset the process, the question of what can be done to improve constructability has to be posed.

Constructability means, basically, being more searching within construction design, so as to develop the effective facets and eliminate the detrimental aspects. This, to a great extent, requires a change in attitudes away from the acceptance of mediocre design solutions and towards striving for superior solutions. This objective, however, must be viewed with the understanding that it is impossible to refine every conceivable aspect of design and that it is practical and not idealised refinement that is sought. Because constructability starts with design, designers must become more sensitive to the implications of their output. Contractors must, not only for the sake of the construction process, but for their own survival give more support to the consideration of design alternatives that can produce simpler and more economic methods of construction. Users must become familiar with the need to provide feed back to designers information regarding any inadequacies in design and construction.

Nor, of course, are designers and contractors always to blame. Many problems emerge from vague forms of contract, clients who misinform or change their minds, or specialist contractors who have little contact with the procurement process, to give but three simple examples. Of course, here we are concerned not with apportioning blame for shortcomings in construction, but with the continued evolution of construction and the vital part played by constructability in that evolution.

Two facts are obvious: first, constructability may be more the product of self-actualisation by the parties than of architectural propositions consciously drawn into the design or of particular management strategies used on site. Given this, it is all the more important to make a more positive effort to implement practical constructability, as clearly there is considerable scope for designing out, and constructing out, through greater sensitivity to the problems, many of the common defects prevalent in the process. Second, constructability is not merely an aspect of design, or of production. Developments in it emerge from analysing feedback from procurement, design, construction and use, making it a total project concept which relies on each and every contributor to the total construction process playing his part.

2.2   Project Aspects Influencing Constructability

Without doubt, constructability is, a multi-faceted and complex subject. In the quest for more constructable buildings, structures or engineering works, constructability will only result when there is a conscious effort to understand and anticipate the problems that occur within the total construction process, not just its isolated aspects. The factors influencing this process are many and varied, and analysis is not merely a question of isolating and defining them, because they overlap and develop complex interrelationships which can be difficult to rationalise. However, if we are to understand constructability at all we must consider the component phases and see just where it can help to ease work within each of them, to the benefit of the whole.

Factors influencing constructability

Factors within the construction process that influence constructability are many, and while some are inherent in all construction projects others are, obviously, generated by those characteristics unique to a particular one.

Constructability may be influenced during the following project stages:

- conceptual planning and procurement;
- design;
- construction (production);
- construction management.

The following must also be considered:

- use of the finished product (operation and maintenance);
- project characteristics (situational and environmental).

Within these, specific aspects influencing constructability can be identified, as follows:

- *Conceptual planning and procurement*
  - understanding the client's corporate objectives;
  - definition of the client's project requirements;
  - definition of the project strategy;
  - identifying and prioritising the project objectives (time, cost, quality, constructability)
  - specification and definitions of authority, responsibilities and relationships.

  The procurement route will determine the contractual approach adopted and therefore will be influenced by the following factors also:
  - consideration of the project risk;
  - selection of an appropriate form of contract;
  - drafting of special conditions of contract;
  - contract negotiations;
  - contract administrative procedures.

- *Design*
  - analysing the design concept and its requirements;
  - specification of materials and components;
  - simplification of construction details;
  - appreciation of the task dependency;
  - incorporation of standardisation;
  - specification of realistic tolerances;
  - dimensional co-ordination of the elements;
  - effective communication of design intentions to the workplace.

- *Production methods*
  - construction knowledge and skills;
  - method of construction;
  - sequence of assembly operations;
  - organisation of trades, specialisations and operative gang sizes;
  - level and deployment of resources;
  - methods of site management and project control;
  - standards and control of workmanship and quality;
  - use of feedback and reporting mechanisms.

- *Construction management*
  - organisational structure;
  - managerial style;
  - industrial relations;
  - methods of planning; progressing and targeting schemes;
  - materials procurement;
  - use of plant, equipment and small tools;
  - site layout;
  - operative planning and control;
  - safety aspects.

- *Use of the finished product*
  - installation and commissioning;
  - operational user requirements of the owner or occupier;
  - expectations of life cycle and life cycle costs;
  - preventive and reactive maintenance requirements.
- *Project characteristics*
  - type: building, civil engineering, heavy engineering, etc.;
  - size of site;
  - location of site and general topography;
  - availability of resources;
  - site conditions including subsoil characteristics;
  - regulations, by-laws and other specific restrictions.

  There are also situational and environmental aspects to consider, these include:
  - prevailing climatic conditions and weather;
  - potential for accidents;
  - effect of human factors;
  - effect of construction on the environment.

It can be seen from simply outlining the broad categories of influential factors just how complex it may be to appreciate the concept of constructability. It is essential that such appreciation is done in this logical way because in so doing, cost appraisal for constructability can be considered along with those technical characteristics that are so important to any project: form, function, performance and aesthetics.

2.3   The construction process

In its widest possible terms of reference constructability remit aims to improve the integration within the total construction process of those parties that combine to procure, brief, design, construct, use and maintain a building or engineering product. Moreover, as a concept it seeks to interrelate the various separate phases of construction to produce a set of principles that are implied and accepted and, inherently, apply constructability thinking to each stage for the benefit of the whole process. Essentially, constructability is usually seen as the contribution that design can make to assist construction work on site (i.e. buildability); but though this is vitally important, and a major part it is only one element in understanding the full concept.

Stages of the process

To appreciate more fully the contribution that constructability can make, it is important to outline briefly what the construction process seeks to achieve.

Since the mid-nineteenth century, the design element of the construction process has increasingly diverged from the construction functions on site. Moreover, construction professionals have also specialised, thus further exacerbating the division. This situation has effectively produced a process in which the designer and the contractor are both unsure as to the other's role and function. In the traditional setting this can only lead to designs that fail to develop the best aspects of construction, and to construction that fails to bring out the best facets of design. In either case, the client ends up with an inferior product. Today's building and engineering technology allows highly complex designs, innovative use of materials, sophisticated plant and equipment, and demands greater management input through more involved contractual systems. The needs of clients who want the best from their project demand that constructability must be considered at each stage in the construction process for real benefits to be achieved, while clients do not want divisions within the process but a greater level of integration and teamwork towards project success.

The feasibility stage

The construction process commences when a client perceives a need for a construction product. The traditional approach is pursued through a feasibility study or an economic appraisal of the client's needs and benefits, taking into account also the many relevant moral, social, environmental and technical constraints. The outline cost of the potential project will be ascertained from a number of possible sources, especially records for similar construction projects. If a feasibility study shows that the objectives of the client are best met through the ideas generated then he will, again traditionally, procure the services of a design and/or engineering consultant to develop his notional ideas into a more workable form.

Traditionally, constructability is not thought of at all at the feasibility phase; yet subsequently it will be seen that modern construction demands that constructability be considered at this early stage. For example, within the client's outline idea of need and requirement constructability can provide feedback from past projects to aid consideration of the current project. Constructability is also concerned with the basic method of procurement and employment of consultants. For example, consideration of constructability can involve evaluating the arrangement of the parties by suggesting the advantages and disadvantages of the traditional route as against design–build, management-based systems or design-and-manage approaches. Constructability can assess not only the technological aspects and potential methods of construction, but also the formal arrangement between the participants.

The briefing stage

Traditionally, design is commissioned on a fee basis or through a bid. The design team's approach will set out the client's requirements in a more formalised way and in some detail on the basis of the functional needs of the user, this being the client's brief. Constructability is a fundamental pre-requisite to a successful brief. The designer should be able not only to provide advice on the planning and legislative requirements, but also to have considerable empathy for the construction consequence of the client's requirements. Constructability is crucially dependent upon the combination of materials and components in any design; therefore, the client's brief and the designer's interpretation of the brief, together with the specification which results, are fundamental to the level of constructability that may be achieved.

The design stage

Once this outline stage is completed satisfactorily, the designer will develop a final sketch design depicting layout, structure, and construction to the client's satisfaction. The consideration of constructability is basic to this phase, as it allows the detailed scrutiny of alternative design solutions and of the ergonomics of layout, both internally and externally, if it is a building; it also helps to determine how the design solution can directly increase ease of construction on site when the work is carried out. Of course, the broad design situation is critical to constructability. A simple, uncomplicated construction using repetitive elements may have a high constructability factor, whereas a bespoke construction project may be intrinsically costly and have a lower factor of constructability because it incorporates innovative materials or requires specialised assembly.

The tendering stage

Traditionally, the work is usually put out to tender using either open or selective procedures. Tendering is, of course, based on project documentation, drawings, specifications and a bill of quantities, and it is within this documentation that constructability can be formally incorporated into the project. If the concept has been considered consciously and seriously throughout the foregoing stages then it is a case of detailing the requirements for constructability within the project documentation, drawings and specification. The requirement for constructability, therefore, forms an integral aspect of the tendering process, and prospective contractors must allow for considerations of constructability in their submitted tenders and assume the responsibility for the implementational aspects during the construction itself. It is this transfer of such considerations from the design to the subsequent construction phase that is crucial in setting the benchmark for good constructability during the latter stage. This, added to the conscious construct-ability imparted by the construction process on site, means that overall the project should have a greater chance of achieving increased constructability. Constructability is dependent not only upon the content of the work through the design and specification but also upon how the work is undertaken. Both of these aspects should reflect constructability in the tender.

The construction phase

During the construction phase, constructability is, of course, primarily the focus and responsibility of the contractor. In translating the requirements of the project documentation, drawings and specifications completed at the design stage, he must impart as much consideration of constructability as possible in undertaking all aspects of the site production process. This means that he also assumes the responsibility for ensuring that general principles of constructability are also carried out by the subcontractors and other provi-ders of specialist inputs to the process. There is also a considerable and continuous onus on the contractor to liaise and work with the design team and other consultants and, moreover, to provide feedback on the construc-tion phase for future analysis and the general betterment of knowledge. The key to effective and efficient constructability on site is good planning, ade-quate resourcing and continuous control, which add up to good general site practice.

The role of building professionals

Constructability strategies and approaches can only be developed if the various building professionals involved in the total construction process make a valid and timely contribution to the overall objectives. Constructabil-ity develops an information loop in which all participants must contribute their skills, expertise and experience to solving problems as they arise within their particular scope and range of contribution: for example, the designer during the briefing and design phase, the quantity surveyor during evaluation phase, the contractor during the construction phase, etc. The contributors of each building professional then combine to form a flow of constructability information throughout the total construction process, which can be further developed to form a feedback channel through every stage. Only in this way is the constructability loop effectively developed.

Each building professional has a vital role to play in developing the construct-ability loop. If the contributor fails to consider constructability within his remit of activity, then essentially the prospect for better constructability across the process will be weakened severely or even completely destroyed. Construct-ability is therefore dependent upon the combined efforts of everyone.

2.4   Constructability: strategies for the construction process

Within construction generally, the clear objectives of the various professionals are to provide satisfaction, quality of service and value for money to the client, while at the same time achieving adequate recompense for their labours. Standing some way apart from this is of course the client, who procures the work in the first instance, and who is often the user or occupier of the completed product, but who, because he employs consultants on his behalf, is somewhat removed from the activities involved.

Constructability is a concept that must seek to alleviate the problems of separation and demarcation between the contractual parties, and the processes involved. Moreover, constructability must seek to resolve the many problems of performance, technology and management that confront the practical construction process. Within the latter, constructability will, if truly recognised, accurately understood and consciously implemented, be able to do the following:

- *Awareness*   Provide a greater awareness of the potential benefits of constructability within the construction project.
- *Dialogue, interaction and teamwork*   Promote continuing dialogue between the client, contractual parties and user of the final product of construction to produce a constructability loop.
- *Principles and standards*   Develop a set of identifiable and easily understood principles and standards for making any construction project more constructable at each stage in the total process, with the main focus upon procurement, design, production and use of the product.
- *Communication*   Encourage closer interrelationships and better liaison and teamwork between the various contractual parties during each phase of construction.
- *Information, knowledge and feedback*   Provide detailed quantitative and qualitative feedback to all parties on the success, or otherwise, of their attempts to enhance constructability for use in their future projects.
- *Education*   Seek to promote constructability as an essential aspect of project briefing, education and on-the-job training provision for each professional discipline and across disciplines within the project team.

Developing strategies for constructability

Strategies must be developed at each phase in the construction process such that benefits are accrued within the phase itself and across the whole process. Strategies must be developed by each and all of the various construction professionals, which are aimed at linking on one hand, the potential benefits in each phase that ostensibly benefit the individual participant with, on the other, the broader benefits across the project, to the betterment of all participants. Constructability challenges all construction professionals to question, perhaps more deeply than ever, what it is they do, and to look with renewed focus and direction upon their relationships with others. The overall aim of a constructability strategy is to stimulate thought among construction professionals and to provide a basis for project teams to apply constructability concepts and principles appropriate to their projects.

References

1. R.Jortberg, *CII improving Constructability*, video of workshop, May 1991, Construction Industry Institute, University of Texas, Austin.
2. A. Griffith, 'A Critical Investigation of Factors Influencing Buildability and Productivity', PhD Thesis, Heriot-Watt University, Edinburgh, 1984, unpublished.
3. R. A. Burgess, 'The Management of Resources on Construction Sites', Building Research Establishment, 1978, Building Note no. 181.
4. H. Emmerson, *Survey of Problems Before the Construction Industry*, A report prepared for the Ministry of Works, HMSO, London, 1962.
5. H. Banwell, *The Placing and Management of Contracts for Building and Civil Engineering Work*, HMSO, London, 1964.
6. Economics Development Council, *Action on the Banwell Report*, HMSO, London, 1967.
7. National Economic Development Office (NEDO) *The Wood Report: The Public Client and the Construction Industry*, HMSO, London, 1975.
8. Construction Industry Research and Information Association (CIRIA), *Buildability: An Assessment*, CIRIA Publications, London, 1983, Special Publication no 26.
9. N. Sidwell, *The Cost of Private Housebuilding in Scotland: A Report for Scottish Housing Advisery Committee*, HMSO, London, 1970.
10. (BRE) *Common Defects in Low-Rise Traditional Housing*, BRE Publications, Watford, 1988.
11. National Economic Development Office (NEDO), *Achieving Quality on Building Sites*, HMSO, London, 1987.

3 Constructability in Conceptual Planning and Procurement

This chapter considers traditional and non-traditional methods of procurement and their implication upon constructability in the context of industry's increasing expectation of innovative and improved procurement strategies.

3.1 Conceptual planning for constructability

Client priorities

In today's extremely competitive construction marketplace, contractors in all sectors, whether general or specialist, must respond to the needs of clients efficiently and effectively and, moreover, give quality of service and value for money. Prior to the mid-1980s the mainstream of the construction industry had followed traditional methods of procurement using long-established forms of contract. Many clients today, however, are increasingly dissatisfied with the traditional approach and its operational characteristics, and actively seek alternative methods of procurement, organisation and management to meet their changing and more exacting needs. It is clear that the method of procurement adopted by clients has a profound influence upon the potential for constructability in modern construction projects.

Client demands

For constructability to be successfully undertaken, its principles and procedures must be well defined and recognised at the beginning of a project. Constructability must form part of conceptual planning and procurement.

Many of today's construction and engineering projects are very costly and highly complex, employing new materials and technologically advanced construction methods. Typically, demands are being made upon the construction process not just in terms of time, cost and quality, but also in those of project organisation, management and procurement.

Clients, in particular those in the private sector, find that they must procure new construction works more rapidly than ever before in striving to remain commercially competitive and to satisfy their own client's or customer's ever-increasing needs. As demands upon clients increase, so the construction industry in general must respond, producing quality work that is inherently more constructable and that provides the best possible performance and value for money. While the design or construction phase of a project can always be made more constructable to some degree, constructability must always be considered in relation to time, cost, quality and other significant project priorities.

Today, many clients know enough of the workings of construction to know what they want and what they may expect in terms of project performance. Some clients are also seeking greater participation in the projects that they procure, and no longer is the client prepared to sit back and be represented exclusively by consultants. Such clients are taking the initiative and are supporting those procurement systems that enable them to have a greater say in the construction process and allow them consciously to impart constructability into their projects.

Conceptual planning

Essentially, clients are looking for a 'best buy' procurement package and they focus therefore on a strategic overview of the benefits that may be available to them in using any particular approach. Moreover, they seek to examine the implications of the procurement form across the total building process to assess overall balanced benefits and advantages.

Choice of procurement by most clients will be based, without doubt, upon their range of knowledge and experience and their resource base. It really depends whether the client wishes to be design-led, has confidence in alternatives such as contractor-led or management-based approaches, or has a requirement for competitive bidding within the confines of the best-buy options available.

Certainly, every client evaluating procurement options has key issues to address. These may be summarised as follows:

- the economic objectives, balancing speed of delivery, quality of service and value for money;
- meeting his genuine design, technological, and user needs, within the economic objectives;
- determining how the building is to be managed through the construction stage, in line with the economic objectives;
- ensuring that the finished product is delivered on time to meet the needs of the user and/or occupier;
- the distribution of cost within the economic objectives, i.e. the flow of finance through the contract.

Constructability must become an integral aspect of project philosophy and concepts as early as possible. The requirements for constructability must be identified at the conceptual stage and must become an important part of the overall project plan. They must reflect the client's genuine needs and address his corporate requirements. While the way in which the client handles this aspect will, obviously, vary from client to client, it is essential that the client seeks to establish an integrated project team. Only in this way will a systematic approach to integrating the various stages of the construction process be achieved and the client's goals and objectives become more assured. Early consideration of constructability is essential, because this will clearly influence the procurement route favoured by the client.

Essential factors for the client to consider at the conceptual planning stage are:

- corporate objectives;
- available resources;
- project team knowledge and skills;
- project and external influences.

Briefing

In the majority of building and engineering projects, the brief will make no explicit reference to constructability requirements. Through specifying his preferences of project priorities, time, cost and quality, etc., the client intrinsically makes decisions that directly affect the level of constructability that is desired, or achievable. According to client priority, the brief should, where possible, explore potential alternatives in technical and managerial solutions in order to enable constructability to be optimised. It is clearly in the client's interest to consider constructability at the earliest possible stage, to ensure that the subsequent design reflects his corporate objectives and the desired level of involvement in the process and promotes the necessary integration and teamwork that gives the project the greatest chance of success.

3.2   Procurement options

The prominent arrangements available to the client for the procurement of construction projects can be broadly grouped into the following classifications, which can accommodate both building works and engineering projects.

- traditional contracting;
- design and construct;
- management-based methods – management contracting;
                             – construction management;
- design and manage – consultant-based project management;
                      – contractor-based project management;

While it is not possible to provide highly accurate indications of client preference for particular procurement methods, it is clear that there has been, since the early to mid-1980s, considerable shift in procurement emphasis. In reviewing various statistics and data, Turner[1] suggests that in 1990 the traditional procurement route accounted for between 50 and 65 per cent of construction work, with design–construct and management-based and/or design-and-management approaches accounting for 15 to 25 per cent and 15 to 20 per cent respectively. Alternative forms of procurement are undoubtedly being supported, and through a number of these the propensity for constructability is improved to some degree. As with any aspect of construction, things simply do not happen because a particular procurement system has been pursued, but rather clients, consultants, contractors and other participants must consciously strive to achieve better constructability and improved performance. The procurement system must be carefully chosen to ensure that the client obtains the approach that will best satisfy the constructability consideration of:

- corporate objectives;
- overall programme;
- integration;
- team skills.

3.3   Traditional contracting

Traditional contracting, where responsibility for the construction design lies exclusively with the client's chosen consultants and the contractor is selected by a responsible tendering process, and only for construction and not design, has been the typical method of procurement for many years. This approach is well understood and has some clear and important advantages. It is usually a sequential process, with the opportunity for decision making and review at discrete stages. It is unequivocal in the allocation of responsibility for design to the consultants and construction to the contractor. The traditional approach facilitates competitive bidding and provides a contractual basis for variations and monitoring the progress of the works. The allocation of risk is clearly defined. However, the traditional approach imposes contractual and temporal segregation between those with actual construction expertise and the design team.

This may be partly overcome by appointing construction consultants during the early feasibility and design stages. Value engineering or value management studies are sometimes undertaken. Where the construction consultant is a contractor who may subsequently be included in the tender list, experience suggests that the contractor may not reveal all his best ideas in case another contractor wins the bidding.

A second option for marrying the benefits of construction expertise with the traditional approach is to invite bidders to submit alternative solutions. This can result in more constructable designs, but brings with it difficulties in the evaluation and comparison of the bids.

A third option allows contractors to suggest and introduce constructability alternatives post-tender, once appointed; however, the ability to influence cost is considerably reduced by this stage.

The traditional approach has, in the eyes of some, been perhaps somewhat dismissive of constructability over the years, and has encouraged a proliferation of alternative procurement approaches. It will be seen subsequently, however, that not all alternative procurement methods lend themselves to improving constructability exclusively; rather, their use meets favourably with the pursuit of other project priorities: cost and time, for example.

Perceived inadequacies of traditional procurement

Some clients have become increasingly dissatisfied, in certain circumstances, with the difficulties and ambiguities in the traditional construction process. With fragmentation in structure and procedures, and also in the relationships between contractual parties, they are now actively seeking new methods of procurement that simplify the formal procedures of construction and concentrate resources and effort to improve performance. While the design and construction functions traditionally have been separate, but clients now increasingly demand a single point of contact in their dealings with the industry; they seek project organisation and management-based upon clearly established roles and responsibilities, and where greater communication and integration within the process are essential prerequisites.

More and more, therefore, clients find traditional procurement somewhat counterproductive to their activities, and in recent years a trend has grown towards supporting more innovative, non-traditional processes of procurement that can, in the right situation, realise far greater rewards.

While conscious separation of the managerial role from design and construction has led to the development of management-based and design–management approaches, 'design–construct' is one alternative to the traditional process which has more recently assumed considerable prominence. It has the potential to meet the aspirations of the many building clients who now avidly pursue better constructability throughout the total building process.

3.4   Design–construct

It is frequently suggested that bringing the whole construction process under a single point of control that is directly responsible to the client can achieve greater overall effectiveness and integration as well as better constructability. Design–construct is one form of procurement directed explicitly towards this objective. Although the concept is not new, it has only emerged as a distinct procurement form since the early to mid-1980s as a result of industry's committed search for better construction solutions.

Design–construct has been said to hold the potential to reduce contractual ambiguity, increase operational efficiency, improve overall constructability and give the client better value of money. However, its emergence has not been trouble free and its growth has been limited by a number of factors, not least of which is its lack of acceptance by some professions within the industry.

Design–construct defined

With the design–construct method of procurement, the client makes an agreement with one single administrative party, usually, though not always, the main contractor, who is given responsibility for the whole project from initial briefing to final completion. Design–construct involves the contracting organisation becoming the overall co-ordinator and manager of the construction team. The Chartered Institute of Building (CIOB) publication *Project Management in Building*,[2] discusses some of the principal; issues of this and other procurement forms and the reader is directed to this work.

Structure

In practice, design–construct procurement is generally structured in one of two ways:

- The client employs a dedicated design–build organisation with its own in-house design team.
- The client engages a general contractor who employs external design consultants as members of the contractor's team for the duration of the project.

The organisation and management structure for a design–construct contract is illustrated in Figure 3.1 and this can be contrasted with the contractual and managerial structure of the traditional procurement approach shown in Figure 3.2.

Design–construct approach

Design–construct procurement commences when the client identifies the need for a building or other construction. The client states the project requirements, referred to in the contract[3] as the 'employer's requirements'. In

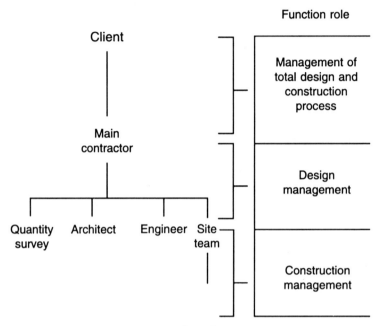

Figure 3.1   *Management structure for a design–construct procurement system*

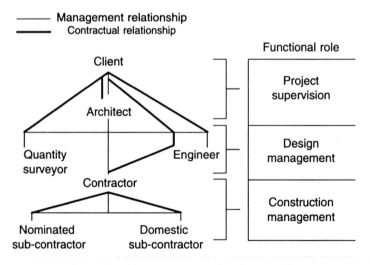

Figure 3.2   *Management structure for a traditional contract*

preparing the employer's requirements the client will usually appoint 'professional advisers' such as an architect and quantity surveyor. The employer's requirements are issued to prospective contractors, who prepare a planned and costed design proposal known as the 'contractor's proposal'. Each proposal submitted is evaluated by the client, and a contractor is selected. The successful contractor prepares a fully detailed design and co-ordinates and manages all aspects of the siteworks through to final completion of the project, an approach that can do much to benefit a project's constructability. The procedures involved in design–construct procurement method is illustrated in Figure 3.3.

Professional advisers

The professional adviser assumes two important functions: first, to assist in clearly specifying the client's objectives, and second, to advise the client with the evaluation of the contractor's proposals. The professional adviser is responsible, therefore, for ensuring that his client obtains value for money and the best constructability possible from the chosen design solution.

Project co-ordination

In most design–construct projects the contractor appoints a 'project co-ordinator' who plays an important role in co-ordinating the various activities at each stage of the project and in establishing effective lines of constructability communication between the professionals involved. Such a person is a vital link in the contractor's organisational structure, ensuring the success of the project through the exercise of sufficient management skill and expertise.

Design team

The design team is directly responsible to the contractor, with a functional line of responsibility to the construction management team. With many projects, the design team is not an integral part of the design–construct organisation, but a consultant employed by the contractor.

Cost control

Project budgeting and cost control are provided by a quantity surveyor, who reports directly to the contractor's project co-ordinator and acts in a functional capacity to the client's professional adviser. At the tendering stage, the client's quantity surveyor (professional adviser), plays a more important role under the traditional system, in that he is continually evaluating the various design alternatives proposed by the tendering contractors in seeking optimum constructability and value for money for the client.

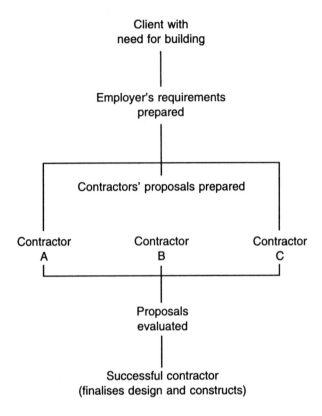

Figure 3.3   The design–construct procurement system

Construction manager

A construction manager leads the project team and reports directly to the project co-ordinator and has a functional relationship with the design team. The construction manager is responsible for the co-ordination and control of all work on site, ensuring that it is to the correct standard and completed to programme in the most constructable way possible.

Client's agent

Forms of contract allow the client to appoint an 'employer's agent', should it so be desired. Partial or total duty and responsibility may be passed to the agent, who in practice may be a design or cost consultant or a clerk of works. The agent is contractually bound and, upon any failing constituting a breach of contract, the employer is liable for damages.

Benefits of design–construct

Design–construct brings a changed dimension to construction procurement, in that it may be said to be structured, primarily in the interests of the client, towards giving an improved deal and with far greater emphasis upon the client obtaining better value for money. These benefits include:

- greater client involvement;
- improved communication;
- closer client–contractor relationship;
- focus on responsibility;
- simpler subcontract arrangements;
- more competent construction practices.

Greater client involvement

As already mentioned, clients in general and particularly the larger organisations, are becoming more knowledgeable in the working practices of the construction industry and are avidly adopting a more active role in building procurement. Because the client is involved from day one he is in the position of selecting the contractor himself, which means that he can select the contractor's proposal that best meets his own corporate and project requirements. In addition, as the client only has to deal with one contractual party, it should inspire greater confidence in the client's ability to contribute effectively to the total building process, rather than assume a traditional passive role.

Improved communication

Because the client is involved from the outset of the project, communication is improved, thereby allowing the contractor to respond quickly and more readily to the client's needs. The client knows who to contact at any time, and in turn the contractor is able to inform the client of exactly what is happening throughout the project. Integration and interchange are thereby encouraged inherently within the system.

Closer client–contractor relationship

Traditional procurement has often been criticised for its inability to integrate the separate design and construction functions. Professional demarcation is a trademark of the traditional approach, ensuring the virtual impossibility of the contractor becoming involved sufficiently early in the procurement process to make any tangible contribution.

Titmus[4] suggests that design–construct meets the aspirations of many clients seeking more innovative procurement. Design–construct provides the necessary multi-disciplinary approach and integration because it forms a designer-contractor 'team' at an early stage in the process, bringing all the professionals and the contractor onto the same side. In contrast, the traditional process separates design from construction through the professionalisation demanded by the contractual form and, rather than encouraging teamwork can create an environment in which the parties tend to defend and uphold their respective 'rights'.

Focus on responsibility

A prominent feature of design–construct is that it provides a single point of responsibility, so that if technological or contractual difficulties arise then the contractor is 'solely' responsible. While traditional procurement may, on occasion, fail to handle design anomalies effectively, with the client more often than not, having to bear the cost of the unforeseen situation, under design–construct the contractor has to ensure that the design is both adequate and constructable, because he is responsible for that design and no design failings can be passed back to the client.

Simpler sub-contract arrangements

With the traditional system, many problems arise from the contractor's contractual relationship with, and co-ordination and management of, subcontractors and suppliers. With design–construct there are no nominated subcontractors or nominated suppliers. This allows the contractor to take full advantage of his own judgement and expertise in procuring only those subcontractors and suppliers with whom he expects to have a successful working relationship. This also holds advantages for the client, because he is not involved at all in the relationship between the subcontractor or supplier and the contractor.

More competent building practices

For projects procured under design–construct contracts there is usually a general requirement to meet fitness for purpose. This is the responsibility of the contractor, who thus is far more conscious of the need to provide adequate, if not considerably better, performance and quality than he would under traditional procurement. The integration and co-ordination of design with the construction process by the contractor can lead to better constructability and should ensure that the ability to translate accurately the design concepts into construction practice will be fully realised. It also enables the

design and construction phases to overlap within the client's overall programme, speeding up the procurement process, which can make significant
savings in time and cost.

Design–construct: its potential advantages over traditional procurement

There appear to be distinct advantages for the client in adopting the design–
build method of procurement;

- Design–construct allocates sole and total responsibility to one party, the
  contractor, and in the event of project difficulty with construction or
  design, the contractor is wholly accountable to the client.
- Design–construct promotes the creation of an integrated design and
  construction 'team'. This improves communication, aids better constructability and directs team work towards satisfying the real interests
  of the client.
- The client can decide which contractor to employ, either by selection or
  by selective competitive tendering. This allows the client to appoint the
  contractor who will best serve the client's technical, financial and other
  needs.
- The client knows, with a reasonable degree of accuracy, the total financial commitment before commencing work on site, because the nature
  of the contract tends to minimise project variations.
- Significant savings in project time are possible through overlapping the
  aspects of design and construction. Design–build can therefore lead to
  considerable savings in cost.
- Closer involvement of the client, designer and contractor leads to more
  constructable and cost-effective design solutions. Emphasis is given to
  meeting the client's genuine needs and to providing value for money.
- The client not only obtains a competitive cost for the project, but also
  has choice of alternative design concepts to meet his needs. Design–
  construct can encourage innovation in design and construction practices.
- Design–construct can encourage a high degree of professionalism. It
  presents a real incentive for the professions involved to work together
  and aim at project success.
- Errors and omissions in design formulation are rectified at the contractor's expense. The client does not suffer financially from the mistakes of
  others.

Limitation in design–construct procurement

In contrast to the advantages, there are a number of discernible limitations
when using design–construct procurement. These include the following.

Discrepancies in documentation

Design–construct relies very much on the continuity between the employer's requirements and the contractor's proposal. Should a discrepancy arise, the contractor may seek to rectify any deficiences in documentation in his own favour.

Insurance cover

In design–construct, the contractor discharges not only the function of construction but also that of design, and this alters fundamentally his obligation with respect to design compared with that in traditional procurement. The client may be at greater risk than under the traditional method, in that the contractor's insurer may not fully appreciate the design risks involved. The contractor may not be adequately covered by indemnity insurance, the extent of which obviously differs as the contractor's obligations change under the different contractual forms.

Client's advisers

Some clients approach design–construct projects without reference to professional advisers. Indeed, the critical role of the professional adviser is little understood and yet it is this adviser who really safeguards the interests of the client. Many design–construct companies encourage their clients to procure professional advice.

Perhaps one of the most difficult aspects for the client, in any type of procurement, is specifying project requirements accurately and clearly. It is within the aspect of performance specification, more than in any other, that the client needs assistance from professional advisers. Professional advice, a vital critical element in choosing any contractual arrangement, is traditionally provided by the designer and so will tend to be absent from design–construct procurement.

Expense of tendering

Compared with traditional procurement, design–construct tendering can be relatively expensive. Contractors usually employ independent consultants for the design and financial aspects which, when added to the additional care and effort involved in producing an accurate proposal, makes the cost of the estimating process high. Many contractors are therefore reluctant to adopt a design–construct approach, fearing the high and unrecoverable overheads on many unsuccessful tendering bids.

Implications for clients

Design–construct procurement presents clear implications for potential users, as follows:

- The development of a clear and concise project brief (employer's requirements) by the client is fundamental to the success of design–construct procurement. Only with a clear statement of the client's intentions can the contractor formulate realistic constructable and financial proposals for meeting the client's needs.
- The client who becomes actively involved throughout all stages of a design–construct project, and who communicates effectively with the contractor, should almost certainly obtain better constructability than a client who does not become involved.
- Unless the client has in-house expertise, a professional adviser or client's agent, or preferably both, should be appointed to see that the client's requirements are met during both design and construction.
- Clients should raise the question of professional indemnity insurance with potential contractors to ensure that the chosen contractor is adequately covered for design liability, since the contractor becomes entirely responsible for design and construction.
- The contractor's proposals should be thoroughly checked to ensure that there are no discrepancies between the contractor's proposals and the employer's requirements. These documents should exist to help constructability and not to hinder it.
- The client should not become involved in design issues, other than stating his initial requirements, and all responsibility should be assumed by the contractor.

Improved constructability through the design–construct approach

To assess the contribution that design–construct procurement can make to improving constructability, the concept of constructability must be looked upon in the broadest sense. Any aspect that makes the project easier to undertake or makes the construction more constructable is a contributing influence upon constructability.

As we saw in Chapter 1, constructability has, in the past, been rationalised to the contribution that design imparts to improving ease of construction (buildability), and yet this is only one aspect of the concept. Constructability encompasses the total building or engineering process, so a contribution towards improving constructability can be and is realised from many project aspects.

From the client's viewpoint, constructability, in practical terms, is concerned with reducing project uncertainty and risk through increasing efficiency in the design and construction processes, simplifying contractual arrangements and improving project organisation and management. Factors influencing time, cost and performance are paramount, because these impinge upon the client's ability to obtain value for money.

Constructability, as a concept throughout the total building or engineering process, has a number of functional aims, and design–construct procurement has the functional ability to fulfil some of them. These are shown in Table 3.1. Viewed from this perspective, design–construct procurement can certainly make a positive contribution towards improving constructability.

Table 3.1   Design–construct: functional ability to fulfil the aims of constructability

Constructability: functional aims	Design–construct: functional ability
Simplified contractual arrangements	Simplifies contractual arrangements: the contract is between the client and the contractor, with total responsibility given to the contractor; and the contractor is responsible for all subcontractors and suppliers.
Integrated design and construction	Promotes an integrated design and construction team in the form of the main contractor. Encourages professionals to work towards the real interests of the client.
Improve communication	Client–contractor single link, and integration of design with construction improve communication between building or engineering team members.
Increased operational efficiency	Significant savings in project time are possible through overlapping design and construction aspects. Pre-construction procurement time greatly reduced and earlier start on site possible.
Reduced cost	Client knows, within a reasonable degree of accuracy, the total financial commitment before commencing work on site. More rapid procure ment also makes cost saving.
Increased performance	Detailed brief, (employer's requirements) and contractor's proposals set out the detailed specifications for design workmanship, materials and performance.
Minimal project changes	Detailed brief reduces likelihood of project changes. If variations occur, contractor can respond quickly and directly to client.

Design–construct and constructability application

From both theoretical and practical viewpoints, design–build has some apparent advantages, but the true benefits can only be realised from successful application. Among a number of studies into the application of constructability in design–construct procurement.[5, 6, 7] most have shown design–construct to be an effective method of procurement which is rapidly finding favour with many clients. Indeed, over 30 per cent of contracting organisations offer a design–construct alternative. Studies suggest that there can be clear advantages to be obtained in terms of simplifying contractual arrangements, better integration of design and construction, improved communication and reduced project time and cost. On the other hand, aspects of performance and quality have raised some concern among clients.

Time

For many clients, time is crucial in forming their perspective of the building process, because for a client 'time costs money'. The NEDO Report *Faster Building for Industry*[8] has emphasised that in most cases, non-traditional procurement methods, including design–construct, tend to be quicker in terms of both site construction time and total project time than traditional methods. Figure 3.4 illustrates the relevant aspects of these findings.

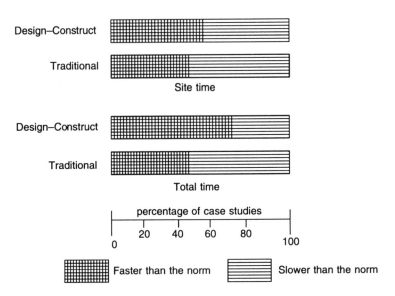

Figure 3.4   Relative site time and total time for design–construct and traditional contracts

Time savings with design–construct are maximised at the pre-contract stage, so the procurement process, up to commencement on site, is much shorter than under traditional procurement. Research by Fitchie,[9] presenting examples of case study projects, indicates that procurement time under a traditional approach can be up to twice as long as that of design–construct. The relative durations of procurement time are shown in Figure 3.5.

These benefits are apparent quite simply because of the ability of design–construct to integrate the project team members, produce open communication and encourage effective co-operation. Given the right conditions and active management, design–construct is definitely a positive contributor to reducing project time.

Cost

While project time is relatively easy to interpret, and potential savings are clearly identified, project cost is more ambiguous and therefore difficult to evaluate. A prominent consideration for the client, in any procurement form, is that the final cost does not exceed the project budget. In this respect, design–construct certainly can present a better chance of the client obtaining his completed project within budget.

Design–construct can be advantageous to the client, since it is known with a reasonable degree of accuracy what the total financial commitment is going to be at the tender stage. In addition, the client knows that there is little likelihood of major variations increasing the project cost.

Cost is, however, greatly influenced by 'degree of risk'. In simple terms, the more complex and difficult the project, the greater the overall risk and hence the higher the cost. On low-risk projects, therefore, design–construct should bring considerable economies through the close link between design and construction, but on difficult and high-risk contracts the contractor must cover risk in the tender, and the cost implications can be severe. Design–construct, therefore, is perhaps not so attractive when project uncertainty is high and when the level of risk to be underwritten by the contractor is excessive.

Quality

A more serious concern sometimes raised by clients in considering design–construct procurement is the ability of the method to ensure quality, both at the design stage and during construction. As the contractor assumes responsibility for design in addition to construction, it has been said that buildings can lose their architectural significance, in an aesthetic sense, as design is integrated with construction. Many believe that the historic separation of design from construction gives traditional procurement a design advantage, and yet, in Bowley's words: 'It is often conveniently forgotten that some of the

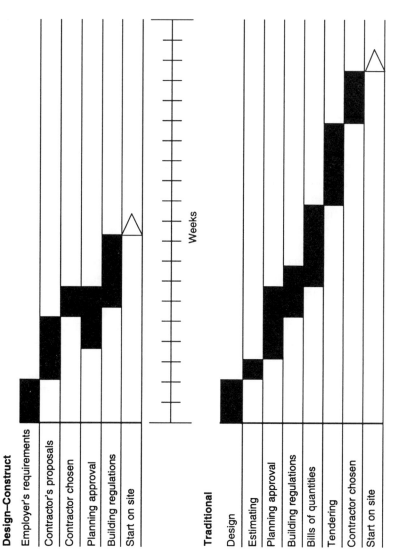

Figure 3.5   Relative procurement times for design–construct and traditional contracts

finest architecture in the country was produced before there was any rigid separation between architects and builders.'[10]

The fact is that, in design–construct, contractors must compete on design as well as on construction price, and this should certainly make contractors more aware of the design aspect. This alone can lead to more innovative and positive design solutions to meet the client's needs. Fitchie found that the total responsibility contractors assume under a design–construct contract tends to make them, and others in the project team, more professional in their outlook and to strive for project success.

Competent performance on site is a further aspect of quality with which the client is fundamentally concerned. The construction industry is frequently criticised for inconsistencies in the provision of quality, and with the increasing interest in obtaining better value for money from the total construction process, the management of procurement and, in particular, the production processes on site are becoming more performance- and quality-oriented.

Design–construct has a considerable ability to improve quality in construction. When procured in isolation, design has always presupposed that the client himself has identified his genuine needs, defined his requirements and specified them clearly, yet, in reality, the client may have little clear definition of what is wanted. In traditional procurement, there is no doubt that clients need greater assistance to define performance and quality in contract documentation. In design–construct, the employer's requirements attempt to ensure that performance and quality are clearly stated and that this is communicated effectively.

In terms of monitoring and controlling performance on site, the client's interests can be safeguarded by employing formal quality assurance systems – a growing trend and one that clients greatly encourage today – and by the employment of a client's agent to monitor day to day activities on site. Design–construct procurement can therefore promote better quality during both the design and the construction stages.

Value for money

To many clients, value for money is probably the most crucial aspect of building procurement. In traditional procurement, the reality of the tendering process is that the lowest bid is almost always selected. In design–construct, the client has the advantage of evaluating contractor's proposals and selecting the one that directly meets his needs and offers the best overall value for money.

Various studies (see notes 4, 5, 9), have shown that clients, in general, express their favour and support for design–construct procurement because, in the right situation, it provides innovative design solutions, integrated organisation and management and open communication, and therefore greater co-ordination, making for better project constructability.

Hybrid variations on design–construct

It has been seen that the overall appeal of design–construct procurement in promoting constructability lies in the quality of its integrated design and construction approach. Contractors tend to favour its use because, while the method may be no more competitive in tendering, it still offers an opportunity to provide a sound service at the same time as making a profit; they also like the method because it gives them command of the total project. However, it has already been said that the change in general attitude and need for involvement by the client have brought new demands on the contractor. It is this interface between the perceived contractor's benefits and the needs of the modern client that can produce potential disharmony in design–construct procurement.

Within the general concept of design–construct, clients now seek to employ their own consultants to develop concept designs, primarily as a safeguard to fulfilling their genuine needs. Contractors therefore have the task of detailing the designs to fit the predetermined concept designs. This sort of hybrid approach can only lead to difficulties, because ostensibly it goes against the grain of the design–construct philosophy where the aim is for greater integration and more flexibility. In such situations the contractor finds that tendering competition is based not on design-and-construct price but rather only on construction costs. Conversely, of course, one could argue that in this way the contractor incurs a lower tendering cost and has the benefit of specialist early design input, but even so such a procedure still defeats the basic philosophy and concept. The clear advantage of such an approach is the earlier involvement of the contractor, and yet the initial design work is undertaken independently by professionals. Earlier involvement of the contractor and subsequent control over final design development can enhance constructability; however, this is depleted in proportion to the degree to which design development occurs before novation.

Because the fundamentally adversarial nature of traditional contracts between client and contractor remains in place under novation, it is unlikely to prove any less litigious. Indeed there are greater risks, owing to the less determinate character of the design brief and the subsequent sharing of risk between the parties.

Novation

Novation is a hybrid form of contractual arrangement that combines the independence of the client-designer relationship in traditional contracting with the integration of design and construct, and it brings some advantages in constructability. Novation is the principle whereby a contract in existence between two or more parties has a new contract substituted for it, either between the same parties or between different ones, the consideration mutually being the discharge of the original contract.

The use of novation in construction contracts allows the client to employ design consultants to prepare a brief and develop the design to the point of legal clarity – perhaps 30 to 80 per cent complete. Once the stage of clarity has been reached, tenders are called, and the successful contractor is then engaged to carry out both the completion of the design and the execution of the works.

Such a hybrid arrangement can pose problems, because neither the designer nor the contractor really knows where he stands in the system unless the contractual arrangement is well developed and specified to accommodate the change in roles and responsibilities. The client also can find this approach difficult, when the contractor attempts to claim against him for problems brought by the designer. Little advantage, therefore, is gained over alternative procurement options; in fact, this hybrid negates the integration and cohesiveness sought by the approach in the first place.

The foregoing is not intended to infer that hybrid variations of design–construct are intrinsically bad *per se* because they are not. Where, for example, hybrid contracts generate more comprehensive detailed design, and the participants understand fully what they are responsible for, then benefits may follow. Traditional design–construct has proved problematic in the past because insufficient detailing of design at an early stage has brought difficulties later in the process. In a similar vein, some contractors have simply not been up to the mark in fulfilling their responsiblities under design-and-construct. Certainly, such hybrids will continue to evolve as clients bring greater demands to the design–build concept and only time and experience will tell if hybrid variations are the route to follow.

Design–construct and constructability: the difficulties of implementation

Lack of professional acceptance

Perhaps the greatest single factor that hinders the growth of design–construct procurement is the required change in the role, the duties and the responsibilities of the professions, combined with their lack of acceptance of this change. The designer, for example, reverts to the role of design team leader, which changes dramatically his relationship with the contractor; from the designer's viewpoint, the contractor becomes his client and the client becomes the contractor's customer. The designer's first duty is to the contractor, and this is a role that many designers may find hard to bear. Responsibilities also change. Cecil[11] suggests that while the designer has a legal responsibility to exercise skill and care, the contractor warrants upon his product a fitness for purpose. The designer should not have any responsibility for the competence of a contractor over whom he has no contractual power. Cecil also raises the point that the designer can become so identified with the contractor that he loses his individual professional status and identity. Therefore, he is extremely reluctant to support the design–construct system.

Lack of promotion

Design–construct contractors are diffident in promoting the advantages of design–construct procurement. This results from the fear of jeopardising relationships with traditional clients and professions. Many contractors are attracted towards design–construct, but in practice choose to respond directly to the client's requirements for contractual arrangement, rather than to encourage clients to adopt a true design–construct approach.

Design–construct presents advantages to the 'informed' client but those clients who have little knowledge of the construction process are still likely to adopt a traditional approach. If design–build is to gain greater support, clients need to be made more aware of the potential benefits. Contractors must become more adept in advertising their ability to meet clients' needs using non-traditional procurement, so that the transition from traditional to more innovative procurement becomes self-perpetuating and the potentialities for better constructability can be realised.

Hybrid forms

The most important thing to watch when using the method is that hybrid variations to approach are developing, and unless these clearly define the roles, duties and responsibilities of the design and construction inputs then their use can certainly detract from the basic philosophy and concept of the pure design–build approach.

Design–construct overview

A multi-disciplinary approach and teamwork are the cornerstones of design–construct. Effective and integrated design–construct procurement, organised around the project team, enables construction professionals to adopt an empathic and constructive approach. Combined, their abilities can achieve much more than when operating from quite separate professional standpoints. This widens the dimension for communication, organisation and management. Clients have become more knowledgeable and involved in the workings of construction, and their attention is now focused upon improved performance, quality and value for money. Design–construct has the potential to produce more innovative and constructable solutions to meet both current and future client expectations.

3.5   Management-based methods

In management-based construction procurement a contractual arrangement is reached whereby particular emphasis is given to the 'management' of the construction process. More specifically, an external organisation is appointed by the client and is paid a fee to co-ordinate, control, and 'manage' the construction phase of the project. The construction works are divided into packages, which are undertaken in a series of construction contracts placed by the management organisation, with the approval of the client, or by the client organisation itself.

The development of management contracts springs from the realisation that the most complex and costly phase of the building process is the construction phase. Therefore, it seems sensible to seek the assistance of those most able and experienced in this phase to work in consort with the client and his design team to effectively manage the construction process. Under traditional contracting the contractor uses his knowledge and skill to complete the project in accordance with the bid conditions but also to maximise profit for his company. There are many circumstances where the contractor can organise more effectively, construct more efficiently and use alternative materials or components. Under management contracts the client buys this expertise and loyalty by engaging the contractor for a fee and bringing him into the team. Subcontractors are still appointed competitively.

Two variations of the general approach exist in practice and are shown in Figures 3.6 and 3.7. These are:

- management contracting;
- construction management.

They are described in practical terms by Janssens[12] as follows:

Management contracting

As the term implies a management contract is one where the contractor is appointed to manage the project, but not build it. The employer and the contractor enter into an agreement with a fixed amount payable to the contractor for the provision of management, common site services and for the contractor's profit. The construction work is undertaken by a series of works contractors, selected jointly by the employer's consultants and the contractor, usually on a competitive basis.

Construction management

With this form of procurement, the construction work is carried out by 'works contractors' employed directly by the employer himself, and hence the employer takes on the contractual position of the main contractor.

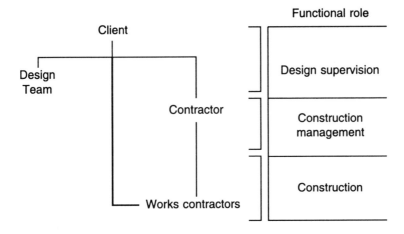

Figure 3.6   *Structure for a construction management approach*

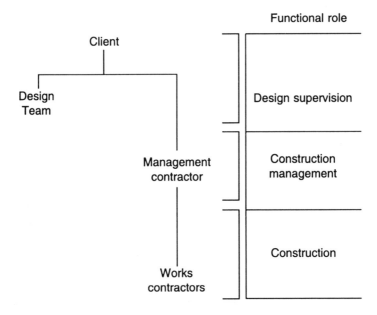

Figure 3.7   *Structure for a management contracting approach*

Since most employers do not have the expertise to manage the works contractor, they employ a construction management firm, on a fee basis, to do this on their behalf.

Direct construction management, or 'contractor CM', is also referred to in the United States under the umbrella term 'construction management', but is known as 'management contracting' in the United Kingdom. The management role is provided by a general contractor, who usually provides the site facilities as well. Trade contracts are made with the general contractor. The contractor may be selected on the basis of tendering on fees, preliminaries and construction time. Often the contractor will provide a guaranteed maximum price, which is established when the documentation is 50 to 90 per cent complete. Costs paid are the actual costs of the trade packages, the site facilities and the management fee.

The essential difference between the two forms of management contracts is the contractual relationship with the trade package – with either the client or the construction manager. A more subtle, and perhaps important constructability issue, is whether the contractor is virtually another professional consultant, possibly removed from the reality of site construction, or a general contractor engaged in the day-to-day hurly-burly of construction activity. Most contruction managers agree that not all personnel reared in the harshly competitive environment of traditional tendering can reorientate themselves to focus on the client's interests first. The advantage of the contractor undertaking both CM and traditional work is the ability offered to transfer staff between the two types, in order not only to optimise their qualities but also to regenerate constructability skills. There is evidence that such management methods have been used in Sweden and the United States since as long ago as the 1950s. Construction management became widely used in the United States towards the end of the 1960s and became the preferred method of contracting for the General Services Administration from 1970 until 1984. The system was introduced into the United Kingdom by Arup Associates for the John Player factory project in Nottingham in 1968, but was modified to have the subcontractors employed by the head contractor rather than the client, and became known as management contracting. Both systems are currently operating in the United Kingdom.

Sidwell and Ireland[13] point out that the construction management (CM) organisation is not always a contractor. They distinguish two forms of construction management, 'agency construction management' and 'direct construction management'. In agency CM the management role is taken by an individual or organisation acting on behalf of the client. Such a service can be provided by a contractor who does other work on a tender or management fee basis, or by a professional consultant. Trade contracts are made directly with the client and site facilities are provided by the CM organisation, or as one of the trade packages of work.

Management-based methods of procurement are appropriate in the following circumstances:

- when the need for early completion of the project is identified as the main priority;
- when the design is not completely defined and described before construction;
- where the client has no in-house management expertise;
- in construction projects which are thought to be complex, or involve high technology or innovative design and construction methods;
- where aspects of the project involve a high degree of risk and uncertainty, or varying requirements are expected throughout the process;
- where the client and/or consultants identify the need to consider particular construction methods during the design phase, i.e. to consider aspects of constructability.

The choice of particular approach, construction management or management contracting is essentially governed by the type, extent and nature of the particular construction project; by the availability of in-house and external design and consultant resources; and by the degree of commitment and responsibility accepted by the client. In Turner's words: 'It is perhaps significant that the element of 'management' should have been separated as 'design' and 'construction' were already separated.'

To some extent such separation seems a natural progression, particularly as long-held views of traditional contracting blame inadequate management as a root cause of deficiencies in construction projects, but this separation of the management function from the design and construction phases only further complicates understanding of constructability. It has long been established that constructability can suffer when the various parties are segregated as in traditional contracting and can demonstrate considerable potential with closer design–construction links as seen in design–build. It follows, therefore, that the separation of the construction parties, for example into works contractors, could be a determining factor in diminishing further the potential for real constructability with management-based systems. This might be true if it were not for the fact that, in such systems, while the process emphasises 'management' of the construction phase, design input is inferred also, thereby allowing an opportunity for constructability to become an integral factor of project formulation.

The greater difficulty is likely to rest in the fact that the contractor or management organisation does not undertake the work but merely 'manages' other contractors (works contractors). While the management of the project may be enhanced, there is greater potential for constructability to be lost in the stretched communication between the design team and what are effectively subcontractors.

Implications for the client

Management-based procurement systems present a number of discernible implications for clients:

- *The clients need to have in-house skills for design – construction or procure the services of consultants.* These methods provide no clear design input, and therefore the client must provide his own detailed brief through in-house preparation or acquire this through costly contracting-out of the design process.
- *Client involvement should be extensive.* Client involvement is inherent in these procurement systems, in particular when construction management is used, as the client enters into many contracts directly with works contractors. This approach is heavily dependent upon client commitment and diligence.
- *The client must identify project priorities and needs very clearly.* While this is a necessity of any construction project, it is particularly pertinent for management-based contracts, because cost and quality constraints are usually less easily controlled than time and progress. The client must be active during the briefing process and identify constructability needs carefully.

The benefits of management-based methods

Constructability is assisted by a number of potential benefits seen in management-based methods of procurement. These include:

- reduced confrontation with the manager;
- early appointment of the contractor;
- contractor selection being based not purely on cost;
- arrangement in contract packages;
- flexibility in design;
- objective selection of works contractors.

Reduced confrontation with the manager

Under traditional lump-sum tendering and other contractual arrangements there is potential confrontation between the general contractor and the client, as the achievement of a high quality of workmanship and of time control will often be to the gain of the client at the expense of the contractor. A bureaucratic and adversarial approach to the management of the contract can also occur, in which the contractor's skills are pitted against those of the client in order to generate claims by the contractor based on weaknesses in the contract. In construction management the CM organisation has little to gain at the expense of the client. If a cost savings sharing agreement is introduced then the CM organisation has a further incentive to save the client money.

Early appointment of contractor

Management-based contracts enable the client to appoint the main contractor (management organisation) earlier in the process than would be the case in traditional contracting. This enables constructability to be considered early on in the total construction process.

Contractor selection not based purely on cost

The main contractor equivalent is selected not only on the fee quoted for management services but also on the proposal presented. A method of work that is selected to meet directly with the aspirations of the design should aid constructability greatly.

Arrangement in contract packages

For projects where design or construction methods are ill-defined, or where project priorities have not been clearly established, management-based methods allow the work to be split into a series of contract packages that best suit the project circumstances. Each such package can be carefully analysed for its constructability facets. Packages may also be developed to evolving client definitions and new criteria introduced to better suit future needs or to compensate for earlier works.

Flexibility in design

Management-based procurement allows some flexibility for design change early in the construction process to perhaps better meet the client's overall needs or to design-in greater constructability.

Objective selection of works contractors

The selection of specialist works contractors is usually, though not exclusively, made jointly between the client's consultants and the management organisation. This can aid organisational interrelationships and improve the potential for constructability considerably.

As Sidwell and Ireland point out, a further benefit is the encouragement of the maximum number of trade-oriented construction bids, resulting in competition. On large projects, the smaller bid packages come within the financial resources of many more contractors. In effect, bidding becomes a more logical process and there is less gambling because there is less guesswork.

Limitations to management-based procurement

In addition to the benefits identified, a number of limitations are apparent in management-based procurement systems. These include:

- *Uncertain project price*   Perhaps the biggest drawback of management-based procurement systems is the lack of an accurate agreed tender price at commencement. Cost only becomes certain as work packages are let and, indeed, some major works packages may not be let until late in the project duration. While this sets a considerable limitation in new build projects, some construction projects, for example maintenance and refurbishment lend themselves to this concept.
- *Absence of specialised knowledge*   Another drawback for management-based methods may arise in specialist works, for example mechanical and electrical services, if the management organisation does not have sufficient technical knowledge or expertise to supervise the work packages on site. Management-based methods require on site management to be well versed in the total construction process, particularly if the constructability achieved is to be the best possible.
- *Restrictive project priorities*   Management-based procurement methods are used generally where time and progress are project priorities, and this can be restrictive where a client requires high-quality workmanship. Quality and cost are often outweighed by constraints of time.
- *Commitment by the management organisation*   Management-based systems are highly dependent upon the skills, dedication and commitment of the management function. Clients may feel that these methods lack commitment to client objectives and cause, especially as the payment is fee based.
- *Over-administration*   There can be a tendency with management-based approaches to 'over-administrate', primarily because of the nature of supervising the many different work packages. Duplication of supervision is likely and difficulties may ensue if the management contractor himself needs to draft in additional skills for specialist supervision. Again, mechanical and electrical services is an example of this requirement.
- *Accountability*   Although standard forms of agreement between owners and CM organisations have been developed, in the event of failure to perform it has proved difficult to determine liability on the part of the CM organisation.

Some public agencies have found that they are unable, legally, to shed or delegate certain responsibilities to the CM organisation. For example the General Services Administration in the USA discovered that certain of their key administrative functions could not be delegated to the CM organisation, and the courts found that the government effectively remained the actual construction manager with the external CM organisation limited to the role of agent.

As we have already seen in the review of design–construct procurement, the prime consideration for the client will focus upon the potential of the procurement system to meet the main project factors of time, cost and quality. Management-based procurement systems must be considered with regard to each of these.

Time

Within the category of time, two aspects are significant; these are:

- *Time savings* Time can be saved by extensive overlap between design and construction. Thus, documentation of the elements requiring early construction can be completed, allowing construction of these items. This has considerable advantages when the overall project time must be reduced, because it facilitates fast-tracking. Data from research by Sidwell[14] shows savings in preconstruction time, construction time and total project time. This would simply not be possible with the traditional approach.
- *Continued evolution of work packages* Management-based methods allow work packages to be continuously developed. This allows the careful assessment of resource allocation to ensure that the project plan and programme retain priority throughout the works.

Cost

Three aspects are significant:

- *Uncertain project cost* As mentioned previously, because work is split into what amounts to uncertain or vaguely specified work packages, total project cost is uncertain. Because firm prices can be obtained for individual packages, and those prices are usually current, at least the prices are, in the main, accurate, up to date and competitive.
- *Lower priority on cost* Because time and programme are the major priorities in management-based approaches, cost may be given less or little priority, and therefore cost control is afforded less management attention.

- *Expensive variations*   The flexibility that management-based methods can allow to the design and construction stages enable variations to be introduced easily, but these are often costly.

Quality and performance

Two contrasting aspects are highly significant:

- *Increased management input*   In principle, there should be closer control of quality and workmanship by management generally, but the fact that the management organisation must supervise a considerable number of works contractors and evolving work packages can make practical, everyday quality control difficult. Quality and constructability can therefore be lost.
- *Lower priority for quality*   In the same way that cost is given lower priority than project time, so too it is likely that quality and general workmanship will be given less attention. Quality control is likely to be outweighed by time and resource management. For this reason, if for no other, it would be advisable for management-based systems to isolate the aspect of quality control and manage quality as a separate quality assurance function, an approach being demonstrated across many construction projects today.

Management-based procurement and constructability

In principle, management-based procurement methods have some intrinsic capability to improve constructability, in particular when the management organisation is employed early in the construction process and with the express intent on the part of the client of allowing constructability to be considered seriously at the design stage. Because design evolves throughout the process, input should be such that there is opportunity to build-in constructability as the work packages are formulated. Case study material,[15] however, does raise some doubt in this area. Forms of contract used in management-based procurement can be restrictive, allowing the contractor to contribute only to the construction phase. In addition, contracts may be vague and may leave ill-defined the role and duties of the management organisation. This can stifle any attempt at proactive involvement at the design stage.

Team approach and combined effort are fundamental to the success of any construction project, and in this regard management-based methods attempt to break down the adversarial attitudes inherent to some degree in traditional contracting by encouraging earlier contractor involvement. This in itself should encourage better constructability by removing some of the traditional bugbears, prejudices and promote common goals. Constructability is firmly dependent upon the contractor being allowed to integrate with the client and designer. Where designer–contractor disquiet occurs in management-based procurement systems, it is more likely to result from a general lack of understanding of the roles of the parties than from traditional professional prejudices surfacing.

It appears that frequently the management organisation is limited in its role by the perception of definition and role held by clients and consultants, and this could lead to the same prejudices that hinder traditional contracting occurring also in management-based systems.

Constructability is highly dependent upon good informal and formal communication, an aspect reviewed in Chapter 5. While good constructability is so often imparted through informal communication at the workplace following close supervision, it is essential that this is backed up by formal communication, and this begins with the briefing and design stage and transpires in the procurement system adopted. Management-based systems, if implemented correctly, can certainly provide the basis for sound communication of constructability concepts.

Research also suggests that the personalities involved are highly significant, and this is particularly so in management-based systems. The way in which each individual understands his role, duties and responsibilities in such non-traditional procurement systems is essential to their success. The perception of responsibility, for example, is vital, because responsibility is perhaps limited and closely defined in one contract, but more loosely specified in another and there is certainly a contrast between management-based methods and design–build and traditional contracting, in terms of the definition of responsibility.

Given the points discussed, detailed investigation by the client and consultants at the management organisation selection stage is, inevitably, of great significance. The client must make certain that the management organisation's general philosophy applies to the project's formal and informal structure, so as to ensure that their attitude is proactive and likely to meet with the aims and objectives of the client team. Only in this way can constructability as a concept be pursued successfully under a management-based procurement system.

Management-based systems: potential advantage over other approaches

With management-based systems a number of discernible advantages appear to emerge:

- *Integration of design and construction*   In principle, if the management organisation is allowed by the client and/or consultant to actively partake in the design process then the same potential benefits that may be accrued in design–build are possible in management-based methods. Improved constructability can result.

- *Shorter duration of the total construction process*   Management-based methods allow potentially earlier completion times to be achieved but only if work packages are closely managed and tightly controlled.
- *Suitable for larger and more complex projects*   Management-based methods lend themselves to larger and more complex construction projects, which require close planning and financial and construction control. This is assumed by the management organisation, and the system allows it to concentrate on the significant project aspects, such as constructability, rather than being enveloped merely in the construction works.
- *Suitable for projects with a high degree of uncertainty*   As the project is carried out in packages, there is a considerable potential for overlap between design and construction where uncertain or ill-defined aspects of the work or changing requirements may be more easily accommodated within the formulation of the specific packages.

The significant aspects of constructability in management-based procurement methods are summarised in Table 3.2.

3.6   Design and management-based methods (project management)

In the words of Turner, 'The "design and manage" system combines some of the characteristics of "design–build" with those of "management". A single firm is appointed after a selection process that perhaps includes some degree of competition on price.' Turner identifies two common variations of design and manage procurement:

- *Contractor-based*   'A project design and management organisation designs and manages the work, generally for a fee, and delivers the project by employing works contractors as its subcontractors to design and/or construct.'
- *Consultant-based*   'A project designer/manager is the client's agent who designs and manages the work, obtains sub-contract tenders from work contractors who then each enter into a direct contract with the client.'

These methods can be broadly termed 'project management', and project management as a concept is one form of non-traditional construction procurement that has increased in popularity since the early 1980s and can certainly demonstrate considerable propensity towards improved constructability. According to Griffith, the objectives of project management can be

Table 3.2 Management-based procurement: functional ability to fulfil the aims of constructability

Constructability: functional aims	Management-based systems: functional ability
Simplified contractual	Although the accent is upon 'management', contracts arrangement can be many and complicated, as management organisation or the client is involved with multiple works contractors
Integrated design and construction	Only promotes integrated design and construction if construction the client and consultants allow early contractor involvement and give free reign in the contract to impart a contribution to constructability at the design stage.
Improved communication	Some management organisations are likely to find that they are merely 'mail boxes' receiving information from design to transmit to contractors. Also, there is a general lack of understanding of management-based methods.
Increased operational efficiency	The project accent towards 'management' efficiency may increase operational efficiency of the methods used on site, but the management organisation's contribution to design process may be limited by client and contractor perceptions of the contract arrangement.
Reduced project duration	Significant savings in pre-construction procurement from an early start on site are made possible as work packages are finished and let as works proceed.
Reduced cost	Accent on time benefits often means cost control is not pursued vigorously. Method of evolving package means that total project cost is not determined accurately and flexibility can influence costly variations.
Increased performance	Again, as time is given priority, quality and performance can be hindered. Performance is dependent upon the many works contractors.
Minimal project changes	A primary aim of the approach is to build-in flexibility for evolving work packages and this inherently means that changes to design, construction and project criteria are likely.

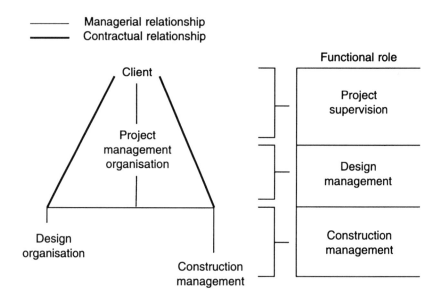

Figure 3.8   Structure for a project management approach

broadly said to be: 'To apply management skills to the structure, organisation and control of all aspects of the construction project and optimise available resources to produce a building that better meets the client's requirements for function, cost time and performance.'[16]

A project management approach essentially separates the management of the work from the construction of the work and acting as the client's agent, the project management organisation represents the client in all matters concerning the project. This leaves the construction professionals free to concentrate on their specialism, the construction, while the project management organisation is free to provide the vital integrating communication, co-ordination and control of the project (see Figure 3.8). A number of publications (see notes 1, 12) review and comment on the design-and-management-based procurement systems available, which the reader should consult at first hand. It is intended here to focus only upon those aspects that affect the potential to achieve constructability.

Depending upon the in-house expertise and experience of the client, the project management organisation may carry out a co-ordinating role under the control of the client (non-executive project management), or may be fully responsible for the management of the work (executive project management).

The general advantage for constructability under a project management approach lies in the simple fact that a project management organisation may be given single and total responsibility for the project, and is therefore able to consider constructability as a concept right through from inception of the works to completion. The integration of the otherwise separate construction phases allows constructability to be identified early, so that those factors that promote it can be built into the design and construction processes. Information regarding constructability is more uniform and there is some degree of feedback throughout the project rather than the usual retrospective analysis of problems that have occurred.

Implications for the client

There are a number of implications for clients when they are adopting design-and-management-based procurement systems:

- *Functional requirements must be well formulated*   The client must know, understand and be able to specify clearly his precise functional needs in order to rely heavily upon one consultant for the design and management of the works.
- *In-house expertise is required*   When integrated design and managerial specialisms are procured by the client through the 'management' function, the client requires some, if not considerable, in-house expertise to provide adequate briefing of his genuine needs.
- *The client should seek involvement*   The client must decide early on in the procurement process just what degree of involvement is to be committed. This is determined by the client's choice of the design-and-management organisation and functions expected.

Design and management-based methods: potential advantages

There appear to be a number of potential advantages in adopting a design-and-manage procurement approach. These include:

- *Focus of responsibility*   The client gives total responsibility to one single administrative party, the design-and-manage consultant, and this provides a focus of responsibility and communication.
- *Integration of design and construction*   The design and management functions are integrated through management, and therefore these aspects should be better co-ordinated and carried out. Construction is, of course, separated from the former functions, but the accent on management means that the works contractors are closely supervised by the design-and-manage organisation.
- *Close co-ordination*   The 'inception to completion' philosophy that is particular to project management orientations provides an open and

perhaps more genuine commitment to constructability teamwork throughout the total construction process.

- *Early managerial involvement*   By definition, the management organisation is appointed early in the procurement process, which produces better integration of the construction and design. Contractors are also brought in at an earlier stage, thereby integrating design, management and construction to a higher degree. Constructability thus, has a better chance of success.
- *Improved communication*   Design-and-management procurement confers a greater propensity for more effective communication. The single focus of responsibility means that the client only has to deal directly with a single party, which assumes the design-and-manage organisation.

Limitations and disadvantages of the design-and-management approach

One major disadvantage, and several limitations, are currently perceived with the use of design-and-management-based procurement methods:

- *Cost*   The great disadvantage for the client in adopting a design–manage approach is that of uncertain financial outlay on a proposed project. Cost is essentially unknown at the time when the client commits to the project. Although an overall cost budget envelope will be known, the exact cost of individual works contractors will become apparent only as works are let by the design–manage organisation and agreed by the client.
- *Limited experience*   A current limitation with design–management procurement is the lack of general experience, so that limited trust and confidence are placed in it, not only by clients but also by contractors and consultants. The implications of this aspect were explored earlier when reviewing design–build procurement (p. 46).
- *Available skills*   In association with the aforementioned limitations, there are, at present, limited skills available in this form of procurement.

Design-and-management organisations may not have all the requisite skills and abilities to 'manage' all aspects of the project to meet the client's exact needs. This is particularly disadvantageous where the works encompass complex technological design requirements, highly serviced buildings, multiple specialised works contractors and the like. On most projects the client will therefore look to a large design–manage team on site to control the project variables closely, perhaps in association with a dedicated in-house team of advisers.

Design and manage procurement and constructability

Project management orientations in procurement demonstrate considerable propensity to improve constructability. Table 3.3 summarises the main points. The key contributor is undoubtedly the single focus of responsibility, and it is this aspect, more than any other, that can increase constructability potential. Constructability relies heavily upon commitment and dedication by the various contractual parties at all stages; this is true of all procurement forms, but particularly for design-and-manage contracts, where there is distinct scope for imparting constructability concepts early on and developing the theme throughout the total construction process.

Once constructability is given recognition in the development of a design–manage project, the 'management' emphasis allows constructability to be transferred from design concepts to construction practice on the site. Paying constant regard to the implementation and monitoring of good constructability during the construction phase means that there should be a high degree of constructability feedback to the design–management organisation and to the client for review, analysis and input to future projects.

As with all procurement systems, constructability potential must be considered within the context of achieveing quality of service and value for money for the client. Certainly, design-and-management-based procurement systems offer a definite potential for improving constructability and, as more clients seek alternative solutions to their procurement problems, this is one particular type of procurement arrangement that is likely to be well supported in the future in larger construction projects.

3.7   Constructability and conceptual planning and procurement: summary, overview and strategies

In recent years many clients, particularly larger organisations, have become more knowledgeable about the workings of the industry, and hold far greater expectations of the building process than ever before. They are attempting to eradicate, or at the very least minimise, the difficulties and ambiguities of traditional procurement and are seeking contractual arrangements based on clearly defined roles and responsibilities, where liability for failure is unequivocal.

Many clients are insisting on more competent performance from contractors, and seek to monitor output and quality standards. Expectations of quality and performance will increase in the years to come, and the adoption of formal procedures to ensure contractor performance and to safeguard the client will become more widespread.

As clients become more demanding so contractors and the professions will need to accept change in their roles and responsibilities. A new form of

Table 3.3   Design and management-based procurement: Functional ability to fulfil the aims of constructability

Constructability: functional aims	Design–management based systems: functional ability
Simplified contractual arrangement	Client deals directly with a single administrative party, the design–management organisation, for design, management and construction supervision.
Integrated design and construction	Overall 'management' emphasis allows design–manage organisations to provide greater integration between the project phases and in-build construct ability to each phase as they progress.
Improved communications	Design–management organisation is free to provide integrating co-ordination, control and communication to all aspects of the project. Client has a single line of communication with the design–management organisation.
Increased operational efficiency	Supervisory element is enhanced but the design, management and construction aspects still depend on the reliability of each input efficiently and effectively integrating with each other within the single management process.
Reduced project duration	Useful approach where the client wishes to start quickly on site, the method retains the element of competitive prices both in the management organisa tion and the contractors.
Reduced cost	Establishing an accurate project cost can be difficult, since cost outlay is uncertain and fees can be variable depending upon circumstances.
Increased performance	The accent is upon control of the three main project variables: time, cost and quality. Performance in terms of workmanship should be achieved given close supervision, but, as always, a detailed brief must deter mine the requirements at the outset.
Minimal project changes	Single line of communication to design, management and construction means that project changes should be effected speedily and comprehensively and at reduced cost.

professionalism will be demanded, based not upon traditional separation of inputs but upon integrated design and construction practices structured around improved communication, more effective organisation and managerial teamwork, and aimed directly at producing products that are more constructable in overall terms.

The prospects for non-traditional forms of procurement are extremely encouraging. The methods satisfy many of the current aspirations of clients for more effective all-round procurement and they meet many facets of the changing face of construction industry as it progresses into the future.

The main points from this chapter can be summarised as follows:

- In certain situations many clients are becoming dissatisfied with traditional procurement and are seeking alternative methods of contract arrangement, organisation and management, to meet their more exacting needs and reduce the potential for project risk.
- Clients, in general, are becoming more knowledgeable about the workings of the construction industry, and are taking positive measures to become more actively involved in procurement. Many clients are no longer distant and uninformed.
- Non-traditional procurement forms have developed considerably in recent years as a result of industry's committed search for better construction solutions.
- Non-traditional procurement can meet the aspirations of some clients through promoting more innovative, integrated and constructive procurement by simplifying contractual arrangements, improving communication and providing more efficient and effective design, project organisation and better construction.
- Non-traditional methods have proved, in some situations, to be significant contributors to improving many aspects of constructability; they can satisfy the client's more genuine needs and can give the client better value for money from the total building process.
- Non-traditional forms have been slow to emerge, primarily because these approaches have not always been supported by some professionals who perceive design–construct, for example, as a direct challenege to their traditional standing, professional status and identity.
- Some clients are insisting upon more novel designs, more effective building solutions and more competent performance from the contractor, and this trend is likely to continue. Non-traditional forms will increase in popularity, as the industry's structure moves towards larger design-and-management firms that have ability, commitment, and professionalism and that will accept total responsibility for the construction projects they undertake.

- It is simply not feasible to prescribe any method of procurement *per se,* since its concept, use and its possible success will rest upon the project's unique characteristics and the client's demands for the project at the time. The ultimate choice of procurement system, therefore, must rest with the client.

Constructability strategy at the procurement phase

Questions

The client should ask the following:

- Does the traditional procurement approach meet all or most project needs, or have difficulties in constructability been encountered in past projects?
- What alternative methods are available with the potential to improve constructability? Are they known and understood (is investigation needed)?
- Could an alternative procurement approach provide any constructability advantage?
- What are the project aims, objectives and priorities (constructability, time, cost, quality, risk, etc.), and how are these managed by the various methods of procurement?
- Which principles of constructability are important to the client (given the priorities) and should therefore be considered?
- Which procurement approach best meets the implementation of constructability principles when these are balanced with other project factors?

Considerations

The client should seek to consider carefully and implement the following aspects of good constructability during the procurement phase (according to priorities determined):

- *Simplifying the contractual arrangement*   Consider the method that will best suit the client's corporate and project needs with regard to his relationship with the designer, consultants and contractor.
- *Integrating design and construction*   Consider the method that will best integrate the design and construction functions and promote constructability teamwork in the project.
- *Improving communication*   Consider the method that will provide the best communication route and determine clear constructability responsibilities.

- *Increasing operational efficiency* Consider the method that will provide the most reliable approach to meeting the project specifications given available resources and construction skills.
- *Reducing project duration* Consider the method that will best suit a early start on site and minimise project duration by considering the overall programme and the programme of individual elements.
- *Reducing cost* Consider the method that will best determine an accurate project cost, balancing constructability with other project determinants.
- *Increasing performance* Consider the method that will best control the main project variables and will best meet overall performance and value for money.
- *Minimising project changes* Consider the method that will best meet the need to accommodate project changes, if required.

Action

To promote constructability within the project the client must at the procurement phase:

- be involved and committed to constructability from the outset;
- be proactive and take the lead in pursuing constructability;
- determine the genuine corporate and project needs (in all their aspects) for balanced constructability consideration;
- clearly identify constructability project criteria and priorities;
- exploit in-house knowledge of constructability and experience (in addition to appointing consultants);
- select the procurement method that suffices constructability principles and that best meets the overall and balanced project requirements, i;e; the 'best-buy' constructability option.

References

1. A. Turner, *Building Procurement*, Macmillan Press, London, 1990.
2. Chartered Institute of Building (CIOB), *Project Management in Building*, CIOB, Ascot, 1988.
3. Joint Contracts Tribunal (JCT) Standard Form of Building Contract with Contractors Design with Amendment 1 (1986) and Amendment 2 (1987), JCT, RIBA, London.
4. P. D. Titmus, 'Design and Build in Practice', *Building Technology and Management*, CIOB (1982).
5. R. Cecil, 'Design and Build: How Successful Is It and How Will It Affect You?', *Architects Journal* (1983), (March).
6. CIRIA, 'A Client's Guide to Design and Build', *Architects Journal* (1985), (March).

7. D. R. Byron, *The Role of the Architect in New Forms of Contracting Services – the Spectre of Design and Build*, RIBA, London, 1980.
8. National Economic Development Office (NEDO), *Faster Building for Industry*, HMSO, London, 1983.
9. J. Fitchie, 'An Examination of the Design and Build Method of Building Procurement', MSc Thesis, Heriot-Watt University, Edinburgh (1986), unpublished.
10. M. Bowley, The British Building Industry, Cambridge University Press, Cambridge, (1966).
11. Cecil, R. 'Professional Liability', *Architects Journal* (1984).
12. D. E. Janssens, *Design–build Explained*, Macmillan Press, London, 1991.
13. A. C. Sidwell, and V. Ireland, 'An International Comparison of Construction Management', *Australian Institute of Building Papers*, vol. 2 (1987).
14. A. C. Sidwell, 'An Evaluation of Management Contracting', *Construction Management and Economics*, vol. 1 (1983).
15. J. G. Connelly, 'Determinants of the Roles and Responsibilities of Management Contractors Compared with Design and Build Contractors', MSc Degree Thesis, Heriot-Watt University, Edinburgh, 1991, unpublished.
16. A. Griffith, *Quality Assurance in Building*, Macmillan Press, London, 1990.

4 Constructability in Design

This chapter considers the potential contribution of the consideration of design to improving constructability, illustrating the concepts involved through practical case studies. Emphasis is placed upon the consideration of design elements and the empathy between design and construction, with a view to producing building and engineering details that not only have greater simplicity in themselves but in so doing are made more easy to construct on site. It should be emphasised, however, that the role of design is primarily to provide design solutions that meet the technical and financial needs of clients. The traditional design process is not focused on the production of the contractor. It is perhaps the responsibility of the contractor to better match the construction process to design needs. Where non-traditional procurement is adopted there is increased opportunity for a beneficial relationship between design and construction. Constructability at the detailed design stage is, obviously, the prerogative of the design team. Consideration of constructability at this stage demands that the following principles are incorporated into the formulation of the technical design solution and its elements:

- construction methodology;
- specification;
- accessibility;
- team skills.

4.1 Design constructability

Definition

Design constructability may be defined as the detailed consideration of design elements to meet the technical and financial requirements of the project, with consideration, where feasible, to the design–construction interrelationship in order to improve design effectiveness and in so doing assist the construction process on site.

Consideration given to improving ease of construction has been practised by a number of exponents.[1-5] Such studies have investigated methods of improving levels of site productivity through the implementation of design rationalisation. While the rationalisation of design has historically been somewhat limited in scope and nature, and has maintained greater affiliation to productivity-oriented analyses rather than it has to explicit investigations of constructability, it has nevertheless provided a base upon which design constructability ideas have been developed.

There can be little doubt that some building and engineering designs are inherently inefficient. Furthermore, many solutions reveal distinctly uneconomic characteristics when it comes to the construction phase on site. This unsatisfactory situation is made all the more so when other designs are seemingly endowed with those qualities that lend themselves towards ease of construction. Distinguishing what makes one design solution more effective than another should be of fundamental concern in the design process.

A first prerequisite for effective design is the evaluation of alternative construction details to assess their relative ease of construction. The initial approach to appraisal is to identify factors affecting constructability for each major element, then to reclassify design types in terms of their individual constructability aspects. Having determined this classification, it should be possible to arrive at some conclusions about the effects of design upon the practicality of construction and enable the justified selection of one design detail in preference to another. The practicalities of construction, as well as financial, functional and aesthetic implications must also be considered. Design constructability cannot be viewed in isolation. Further development of these principles could recognise those factors influencing constructability for many other construction elements. This will provide the facility for tentatively comparing alternative whole buildings or engineering designs in the future.

4.2   Design factors influencing constructability

Any potential design is conceived with due consideration to those factors that the designer or engineer believes to be an important influence over the ease of construction on site. These considerations, however, may not focus directly upon the inherent properties of the design itself, but may, rather, centre around essential but diverse and variable factors, including subsoil conditions, expertise on site, available resources and supply of materials, to name but a few. While these factors are justifiably considered, there are a number of common influences that should be appreciated both with a view to the practical approach to construction and as regards the implications of the design upon cost.

The principal factors influencing design constructability may be summarised as follows:

- level of complexity in design detail;
- accuracy required in setting out;
- interrelationship of different construction elements components and materials;
- complexity of the operational sequence and the skills required;
- flexibility of design and leeway within design detail for materials, components, plant, and craft tolerances.

All of these factors, and more, must always be given due consideration and respect when designing for safe construction. Safety must be a principal consideration on any construction site.

4.3   Constructability in design

This section focuses upon the consideration of constructability principles in design with reference to a range of practical case study examples drawn from applications in building, civil engineering, building services engineering and refurbishment work. Each example reviews a specific construction feature or issue exemplifying the consideration of the principal constructability factors involved.

An extensive two-storey office building constructed on ground with varying subsoil conditions

This case study example focuses upon the substructure design elements of a low-rise, traditionally built office building where the subsoil ground conditions were variable across the construction site. The chosen design solution sought to propose a common foundation detail that would accommodate the variability in subsoil conditions. It highlights the importance of simplifying design elements and reducing the complexity of the operational sequence and the trades required.

Background

Figure 4.1a shows a longitudinal section through the base and soil conditions a two-storey office building, where the foundation detail must accommodate varied ground conditions ranging from sandstone strata to thick clay soil. The building is 90 metres in length, traditionally built in brick-block cavity wall construction.

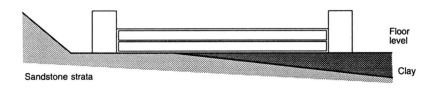

Figure 4.1a   Elevation of a proposed building, illustrating the condition of varying sub-soil across the site

Design considerations

Two design solutions were considered for the foundation elements. The first was to utilise a traditional concrete strip foundation for approximately one-half of the elevation length and make a transition to trench–fill design for the remaining foundation length; the second was to use trench-fill construction for the entire length of the building (Figure 4.1b).

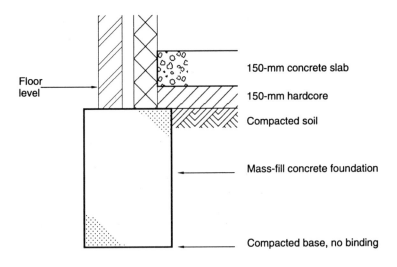

Floor level

150-mm concrete slab

150-mm hardcore

Compacted soil

Mass-fill concrete foundation

Compacted base, no binding

Figure 4.1b   Trench-fill foundation as the chosen design solution

Chosen design solution

The trench–fill design solution was chosen as a common detail for the entire foundation construction. This design proved to be over 50 per cent more cost-effective than the alternative proposal. Constructability is enhanced in the trench–fill design, compared with a traditional strip foundation, as the number of construction operations is reduced, trade interrelationships are simplified and the constituent design elements and the construction operations involved are simpler to carry out. It was discovered in the course of undertaking the construction that additional accuracy was needed in setting out the works, but this was greatly outweighed by the time and cost savings of the lower complexity inherent to the design.

A multi-storey office and residential building constructed in soft subsoil conditions requiring piling

The focus of this case study example is the consideration given to concrete piling and pile head design for a multi-storey office and residential building constructed in soft subsoil conditions. It identifies the pertinence of examining alternative design solutions with a view to promoting standardisation and repetition.

Background

This eleven-storey building comprised a reinforced *in situ* concrete frame with infill brick panel superstructure enclosure.

Design consideration

The designer identified the need for a piled foundation design from site investigation information and chose the principal design concept of driven concrete piles. The consideration of constructability focused on the design detail of the pile heads. Given that the piles were spaced quite closely, the efficacy of incorporating traditional pile caps and load-distributing ground beams was evaluated.

Chosen design solution

The design solution considered to be most effective was to drive precast reinforced concrete piles to bearing depth, reform the pile heads and, rather than cap each pile individually, utilise a reinforced concrete ground beam to link the piles into a composite pile-and-beam foundation (Figure 4.2). This met the structural requirements and also standardised the pile head treatment, aiding simplicity and repetition. A 20 per cent cost saving was suggested in this application.

Construction of machine bases within a petrochemical facility where access is limited

This case study examines the design of reinforced *in situ* concrete machine bases to be constructed within part of a petrochemical process plant where, because of existing production equipment and the layout of the facility, access was limited. It highlights the importance of adopting novel and alternative design and construction methods to encourage better constructability.

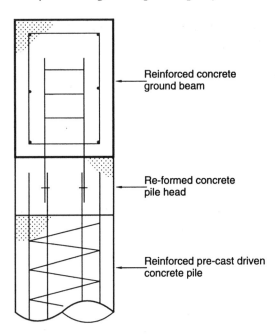

Reinforced concrete ground beam

Re-formed concrete pile head

Reinforced pre-cast driven concrete pile

Figure 4.2   Section through a reinforced concrete ground beam and its link to a pre-cast concrete driven pile

Background

The client, a large petrochemical organisation, required, as part of its long-term arrangement with its principal contractor, a large number of heavy machine bases for new process equipment. The siting of these bases was crucial to the production facility but was made problematic by the layout of the existing plant buildings and the machinery and plant involved in the production process. Shutting down the on going process or modifying the existing buildings was ruled out as cost-prohibitive. The design and construction methods employed by the contractor in meeting the client's requirements were therefore very important to the continuing production processes (Figure 4.3a).

Design considerations

A conventional, large, reinforced *in situ* concrete machine plinth design was considered inappropriate in the situation, because existing concrete bases, plinths and the existing equipment that they supported precluded the construction of a simple rectangular block support. The proposed bases had to be sufficient to provide support for machinery with unequal distribution of load

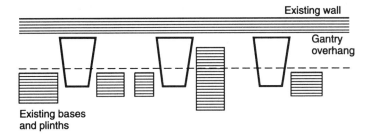

Figure 4.3a   Proposed location of new machine bases within an existing production facility

and fit within the very limited space available. To compound the issue, twenty-four new machine bases were required within the existing production facility.

Chosen design solution

The design proposal was to use a trapezoidal shaped *in situ* concrete base with two short upstand columns, with the inner upstand taking the heaviest load (Figure 4.3b). This could be located within the free floor space available and allow sufficient room to hoist the equipment into position (Figure 4.3a and b). This solution is, of course, standard engineering design, but constructability played a part in the construction methods chosen. Because limited working space precluded traditional timber formwork, two specially made steel forms were used that could be quickly assembled and bolted into position. These could be reused quickly and, more importantly, alleviated

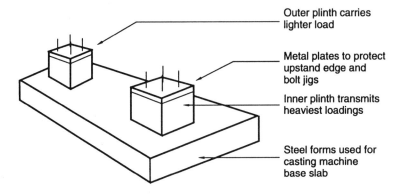

Figure 4.3b   Trapezoidal machine base for construction in a confined situation

difficult trade operations in and around a most restricted site. An interesting feature of the finished construction was that the contractor, having previous experience of the installation process, designed-in a metal crash plate at the top of each stand because they were prone to damage as the machinery was hoisted and slung into position. Substantial time and cost savings were achieved as a result of this approach and, of course, there was no shutdown of the production plant processes, an unquantifiable but important aspect of the design solution chosen.

Redevelopment work on a multi-storey, concrete-framed commercial building in a city-centre location

This case study illustrates the consideration of constructability factors in the design of redevelopment work to a large concrete-framed commercial building. The example illustration focuses on the simplification of beam design to assist practical working tolerances to be achieved.

Background

The case study project was an *in situ* concrete-framed building, seven storeys in height extending an existing framed building by increasing the plan area and the building's height.

Design considerations

In almost all concrete-framed buildings the existence of joints between structural members necessitates the incorporation of heavy steel reinforcing cages, which must be cranked at their ends to meet the fixing requirement at intersections. In this case study, the designer adopted a variation on standard design to allow the contractor greater flexibility in tolerances during the construction processes and to assist in the communication process by simplifying the reinforcement schedules and processes involved.

Chosen design solution

Figure 4.4a illustrates the traditionally designed construction joint at the intersection between two structural beam members. It is common practice to interlock the bar reinforcement cages by cranking the bars and tying them in, using spacers to maintain the required cover of concrete between the formwork and the reinforcement. In the chosen design (Figure 4.4b), the designer incorporated straight reinforcing bars, which by offsetting the cases could be located to give the required cover but without the need for cranking the tie-rods. The designer agreed that the beams did require a minor degree of over-designing to accommodate the extra width and provide the additional

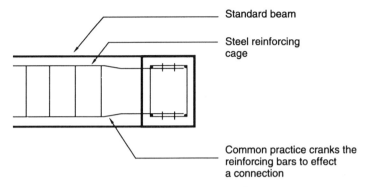

Figure 4.4a   Standard detail for in situ concrete beam interconnection

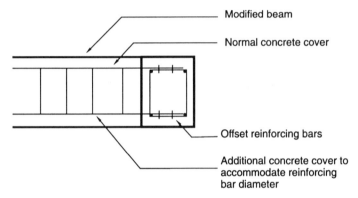

Figure 4.4b   Modified detail for in situ concrete beam interconnection

practical tolerance, but this was outweighed by the ease and additional speed of construction. In addition, problems of insufficient concrete cover, which had presented difficulties in one of the designer's previous projects, were overcome. Taking into account the cost of additional formwork and concrete, but allowing for the faster rate of construction, a 5 per cent saving overall was suggested.

Refurbishment work to a steel-framed warehousing complex

This case study example focuses upon the choice of fire protection measures for a steel framed warehousing complex where a change in the use of the buildings necessitated refurbishment works and, in particular, the upgrade of fire protection to the structural steel frame. This example considers the complexity of the work sequence and the associated task dependency.

Background

The project involved construction works to four large, steel-framed ware-houses on an industrial estate site. The warehouse buildings had been unused for some time and in order to make them fit for occupation again the client was advised to contract an upgrade of the facilities.

Design considerations

The steel frame of the existing warehouses had a minimum degree of fire protection from a sprayed vermiculite cement coating, but past use of the buildings had damaged this on the columns to the point where it was considered that it would be unsafe to leave it pending the reuse of the warehouses. Three alternatives were considered for the works: first, enhance-ment of the existing fire protection measures, using lightweight vermiculite plaster rendered on an expanded wire cage to give a minimum of two hours' protection against fire; second, traditional concrete encasement; third, tradi-tional brickwork to case-in the steelwork. All would provide for the essential fire protection requirement.

Chosen design solution

The design solution chosen was to build traditional brickwork encasement to the columns. This method provided the most cost effective and constructable solution in the prevailing situation. The principal advantage of using brickwork was that it required the input of a single construction trade. Had the concrete or vermiculite options been used, there would have been a sequence of operations conducted by separate trades. In addition, brickwork could be built around the columns without the worry of narrow construction toler-ances, as the brickwork had the benefit of allowing more than adequate protection in addition to the existing vermiculite coating on the steelwork (Figure 4.5a–c).

Mechanical and electrical services provision within a steel-portal-framed educational building

This case study example centres upon the provision of services access within the steel portal frame design of a technical college building. It illustrates the importance that should be given to thorough investigation for improved constructability and the increased simplicity of work on site that can follow.

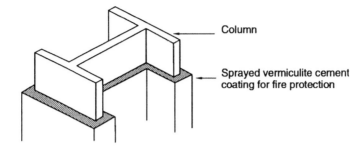

Figure 4.5a   Detail of column fire protection using sprayed vermiculite

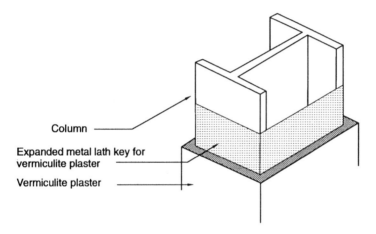

Figure 4.5b   Detail of column fire protection using vermiculite plaster

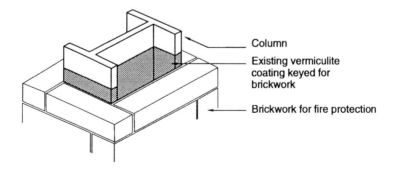

Figure 4.5c   Detail of column fire protection using brickwork

Background

In designing this college building the architect had to be able to accommodate ducts for services and air conditioning within the structural frame, given that the design had minimum floor depths.

Design considerations

In most designs of this type, it is customary to assemble the structural frame and then return later to the need for accommodating services access by cutting holes through the frame and finishes to assemble air ducts and service conduits. This approach usually prevails because at the time of designing the main elements there is usually insufficient information available to the designer to accurately determine their fixed positions. In this project, the designer consciously decided to incorporate the services and duct access into the fabrication process by designing them into the structural frame prefabrication drawings (Figure 4.6a and b).

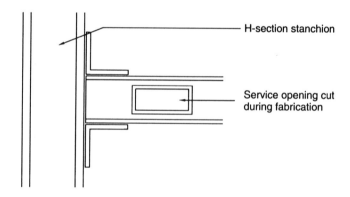

Figure 4.6a   Detail for services opening cut in a steel beam during fabrication

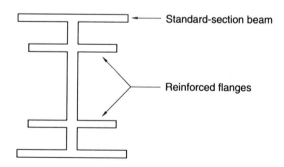

Figure 4.6b   Section through I beam illustrating reinforced flanges

Chosen design solution

In the chosen design solution, the architect detailed service accesses into the steel portal frame elements, reinforcing the access holes with substantial steel flanges. Pre-design work relied upon thorough investigation to ascertain the likely services requirement and considerable design liaison with the mechanical and electrical services consultant appointed to the design phase. This design solution proved beneficial on site, because the need for the remedial cutting of holes was reduced substantially, although, it should be said, not entirely.

Alteration works to a city-centre major department store to provide additional sanitary services

This case study example illustrates a number of constructability principles in the undertaking of alteration works to a department store for the installation of additional sanitary services. Consideration exemplifies the practical sequencing of operations, the simplification of the construction method and the benefits of allowing for practical trade tolerances.

Background

The alteration works involved providing additional sanitary facilities for public use on the fifth floor of a busy department store. These were essential to meet the requirements of additional public traffic within the store generally and in particular for users of the fifth-floor cafeteria.

Design considerations

The principal consideration focused upon generating a design that would simplify the construction methods on site and keep the sequence of operations to a minimum. The key to achieving these two objectives relied upon minimising the input of wet trades in favour of prefabricated components that could be quickly and easily assembled on site (Figure 4.7).

Chosen design solution

Whereas previous alteration works within the store had utilised solid partition walling in lightweight blockwork finished with plasterwork, it was suggested that prefabricated cubicle partitioning be adopted. Remedial works to the washroom walls involved patching up and preparing surfaces for finishing in ceramic tiles. The significant aspect in the cubicle installation was the use of integrated plumbing kits fitted at the prefabrication stage and simply plumbed in on site with flexible couplings. This eliminated many of the traditional assembly operations on site. As prefabrication was used on the

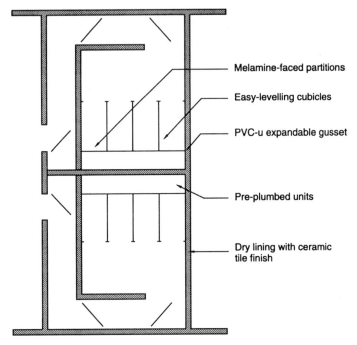

Figure 4.7   Layout of the constituent elements for alteration works for additional sanitary facilities

cubicle units there could be no certainty that fixing on site would not be problematic if assembly tolerances were not considerable, so to alleviate potential difficulty the cubicle units were designed to incorporate levelling screws to locate them in their approximate position. Any gaps were taken up in pvc-u finishing laths, which clipped in position on the cubicle edges and flexed to close the surface.

Underground services to an industrial estate complex

This case study example reviews the potential of a common trench design for services installations. It highlights the benefits of closely interrelating similar construction operations and sequences to entrance constructability.

Background

The construction works involved the provision of multiple services to a series of buildings on an industrial estate complex. Services to be accommodated in the works included: a water main; gas and electricity conduits; and a telephone cabling system.

Design considerations

The principal consideration involved the potential for reducing the separate provision of service trenches. Traditionally, one service run would occupy one trench, leading to the repetition of construction operations with many trenches being redug or dug in close proximity for service installation.

Chosen design solution

Figure 4.8 illustrates the design of a common service trench in which multiple services are installed. By phasing the installation of service runs in this way excavation works are, obviously, reduced to a single operation, and backfill is rationalised to three main operations as each layer of services are accommodated within the trench. On the project reviewed the cost saving was thought to be around 45 per cent on the cost of a separate series of services trench works.

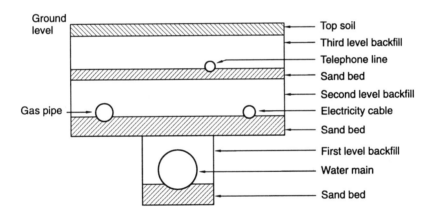

Figure 4.8   Common trench design for multiple building services

Repair and alteration works to a large industrial water treatment plant

This case study example focuses upon the undertaking of repairs and alterations to the structural elements of a water treatment plant. It illustrates the importance of considering innovative approaches to construction methods in order to enhance project constructability.

Background

Figure 4.9 illustrates the layout of a holding reservoir for water used in the process of water treatment within a large industrial complex. The problem was to effect repair works to parts of the retaining wall of the holding reservoir, without having to close down a substantial part of the plant and drain the reservoir.

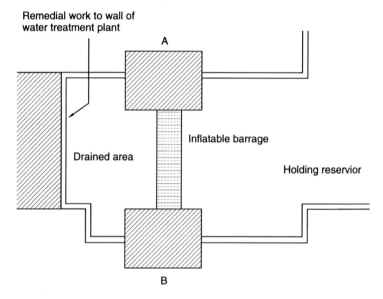

Figure 4.9   *Detail of inflatable barrage used to facilitate alteration works to the holding pond*

Design considerations

Two options were considered initially, the first being to shut down the plant and drain the holding reservoir. This could be done, but not without severe disruption to the continuing processes. The second was to build and fix a jig between the plant buildings, marked A and B in Figure 4.9, and slide into place closely interlocking steel piles, sealing the extremities into the concrete at toe and edges to keep the water out and drain the work area. Continuous pumping would be needed to remove the water that would be likely to seep through the retainment. Subsequently, an innovative method was utilised.

Chosen design solution

The method chosen was to insert a inflatable barrage made from waterproof polypropylene across the holding reservoir and pump out the work area. It was determined that this approach reduced the cost by half, compared with the steel piling alternative. In addition, there was little time lost in the construction processes and, of course, there was minimal disruption to the ongoing plant processes.

Installation of large-diameter pipework under an urban motorway using pipe-jacking techniques

The focus of this case study is the pipe-jacking of large-diameter pipes beneath the four lane carriageway of a busy urban motorway linking a brine reservoir with installations on a large petrochemical processing facility. It illustrates the importance of considering alternative construction methods to reduce complexity in tasks and trades.

Background

The client, a large petrochemical industry organisation, was confronted with the problem of supplying brine from its new reservoir to part of a processing installation separated by a major urban motorway. The design called for a supply pipe 1.80m in diameter. The problem was compounded by the fact that the urban motorway link involved served as a key arterial route for local and bypassing traffic and traffic flow therefore needed to be ensured.

Design considerations

The first design solution suggested that it might be feasible to excavate and lay the pipework using traditional methods, by working across one carriageway of the motorway at a time using contraflow traffic management. However, the local authority highways engineering department did not support this view and requested the client to re-evaluate the routing of the brine main.

Chosen design solution

To reroute the brine main would have been difficult, given the surrounding topography and environment. Also, the additional cost likely to be incurred as a result of a rerouting meant that alternative methods to cross the motorway became attractive. Following detailed site and soil investigations, the method suggested to overcome the difficulties was to hydraulically jack the 1.80 m diameter pipes underneath the carriageways of the motorway. This was

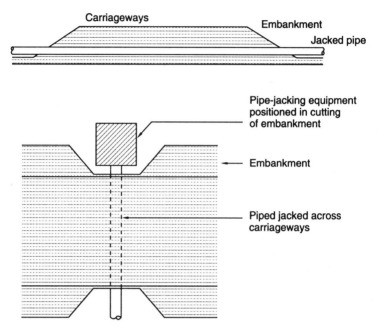

Figure 4.10   Illustration of section and layout for pipejacking through the carriageway embankment

undertaken with jacking equipment strategically positioned in an access cut out of the road embankment. Following the pushing of pilot rods through the embankment, short length pipes were jacked into position and pushed through. This solution proved to be enormously successful. Although considerable time was consumed in setting up the specialist equipment, this was easily outweighed by the simplicity of the construction methods involved and the simplified operational sequences. The total construction sequence lasted three weeks and while traditional excavation methods might have been completed within a similar time frame, it would certainly have caused considerable disruption with major roadworks. In addition, a period of inclement weather which might have severely affected traditional excavation works had no effect on the pipe-jacking operations.

4.4   Design constructability: summary, overview and strategies

The example design variations reviewed confirm that careful consideration of alternative design details and greater empathy between design and construction can achieve improved constructability. The basic principles illustrated may be used as a basis to examine other design elements, in particular more technically complex designs, and to promote the consideration of construct-ability with regard to complete construction projects.

The main aspects of the consideration of constructability in design can be summarised as follows:

- The analysis of alternative design solutions is a positive contribution to increasing ease of construction. Distinguishing those characteristics that make one particular design solution more effective than another is a fundamental prerequisite to good constructability.
- Factors inherent in design that influence ease of construction and that form the basis for considering design constructability are:
  - level of complexity;
  - accuracy;
  - interrelationships between construction elements and between materials;
  - complexity of operational sequence;
  - degree of flexibility for tolerances;

- Alternative design solutions can be identified in many construction elements. The examples illustrate that considerable savings in terms of time and cost are potentially available. While average reductions through adopting a particular alternative design may lie between 5 to 20 per cent, specific elements may in certain circumstances, be up to 50 per cent more economic and practical to construct.

Making a project easier to construct is, in the first instance, a problem that must be addressed during the design process. Constructability is a problem of transforming the designer's conceived picture of the construction into design elements and construction operations that the operative at the workplace can easily understand and follow. In practical terms alone, if the operative cannot construct the intended design easily then the design might be con-sidered ineffective.

Opportunities for improving constructability, from the design aspect, is likely to follow not only the simplification of the technological aspect of the design detail, but in addition from appreciating the sequence of operations and trade interrelationships on site (site constructability). More obvious ideas leading to improvement involve unifying the choice of materials because designs incorporating many different types of materials are likely to lead to problems of co-ordination. Increased use of components prefabricated off site is one potential solution, although this brings problems of off-site manage-ment. While quality standards are likely to improve through improved the consideration of design, it should be borne in mind that improvements may be accompanied by self-made problems. One such problem is perhaps the requirement for more restrictive craft and material tolerances as a result of increased co-ordination in design. Therefore, consideration must be towards obtaining a balance between the practical and impractical.

Constructability strategy at the design phase

Questions

The designer should ask the following:

- Does the designer fully appreciate the constructability needs and desires of the client?
- Are the client's genuine requirements accurately reflected in the design concept?
- Has constructability been fully considered within the design concept and its details?
- Are the design details as simple as practicality will allow, so as to promote design effectiveness and facilitate ease construction on site, or could they be made more easy with further thought?
- How is design constructability best communicated to the client, the other consultants, the contractor and the workforce?

Considerations

The designer should seek to consider carefully and to implement the following aspects of good constructability during the design phase (where it is feasible and practical to do so):

- simplify design details towards more simple construction on site;
- design for the construction skills and expertise available;
- design for practical and simple sequences of construction operations;
- design for practical trade and/or material tolerances at the workplace;
- design for the use of standardisation and maximum repetition, where appropriate;
- design for simplified trade demands;
- design for easy communication to the contractor and/or the workplace.

These represent the minimum design principles. The list is not exhaustive; see the design principles propounded by CIRIA given in Chapter 1 for more detailed review.

Action

To promote constructability within the design phase the designer must:

- liaise closely with the client to discuss the requirements for constructability;
- accurately translate the client's brief into design details taking into account constructability as identified;
- carefully consider constructability within the details when drawn;
- review design details, rationalise, and attempt to make easier the construction on site;
- communicate constructability principles openly and clearly to all parties;
- promote dialogue with the contractor to encourage feedback on design constructability concepts.

Naturally, an overriding concern must be that constructability consideration must be given within the economic objectives of the project. The cost-effectiveness of design analysis must be considered by the client and/or designer and propounded only where it is, on balance, beneficial and effective to do so with adequate regard to the overall objectives and strategy. Being an iterative process, design will to some extent embody the virtues of constructability, but constructability demands commitment beyond mere intrinsic contribution: it requires the client and his designer to commit themselves to it consciously and avidly pursue its concepts. Such commitment is essential, because design largely determines the construction process and what the project will cost.

The pursuit of constructability must be unequivocal and begin early in the design process, because the cost penalties for changes in design increase as the design process evolves. One further considerable advantage of seeking constructability in design is that, in the past, design feedback has perhaps been limited and haphazard, whereas the rigour of the consideration of constructability can play an essential role in making design analysis, recording and feedback more structured and therefore more effective.

References

1. Scottish Development Department (SDD), 'Pitcoudie Housing Developments Phase I & II', SDD Internal Note, 1982 unpublished.
2. Scottish Development Department (SDD), 'Site Productivity for Housing: Blantyre Report', SDD Internal Note, 1977, unpublished.
3. Scottish Development Department (SDD), 'Housebuilding Productivity: Interim Report on the Greenfield Estate, Glasgow', SDD Internal Note, 1977, unpublished.
4. A. Griffith, 'Buildability: The Effect of Design and Management on Construction', Heriot-Watt University/SERC Research dissemination publication, Edinburgh, 1985.
5. N. Sidwell, *The Cost of Private House Building in Scotland: A Report for the Scottish Housing Advisery Committee*, HMSO, 1970.

5 Constructability in the Construction Phase

Unlike manufacturing industry, where an organisation is likely to design, resource and construct its product in one place, or in a small number of neighbouring locations, the construction industry is faced with a completely different logistical problem, because, as we know, each construction project and each production site is set up in a new place each time to construct a one-off product. Virtually every building or engineering project is in itself a prototype, and it is well recognised and accepted that this presents many diverse implications and problems resulting from, perhaps, the remoteness of the site, the availability of the resources and even the climatic conditions, all of which are exacerbated by the various contractual relationships and the high degree of operational mobility and turnover of staff that is prevalent within the industry generally. A wide range of issues evolving from these characteristics presents particular problems to the practical implementation of constructability within modern construction projects. This chapter identifies the criteria that must be considered when constructability is being implemented prior to and during the construction phase. As before, the concepts explored in this chapter are amplified through illustrative examples.

The construction phase

Constructability issues

Two aspects of constructability are highly significant within the construction phase; these are:

- *The direct transfer of 'design constructability' concepts to the construction phase* Design constructability may have suggested particular concepts of constructability, for example modular co-ordination. These must be successfully incorporated into the construction work on site.
- *The implementation of 'site constructability' concepts both before work commences and during the construction work on site* These aspects address organisation and management attributes to improve constructability onsite, i.e. they focus upon good site practices.

Research[1, 2, 3] has shown that while design analysis is essential to improved constructability, site organisational and managerial factors are equally fundamental prerequisites for achieving good constructability. It is well recognised that while good design can never compensate for inadequate management on site, good site management is able to overcome some shortcomings in design if they occur. Moreover, the combination of good constructability during both the design and construction phases can only bring benefits and rewards to overall project constructability. Each is therefore complementary and vital; hence the need for constructability to meet the two basic aspects previously stated.

Constructability criteria

The main constructability principles for consideration during the construction phase are:

- construction knowledge;
- site performance;
- innovation;
- accessibility.

These principles should be considered within the following project aspects (Figure 5.1):

- contractor's responsibilities (within the contractual arrangement between the parties);
- design solution;
- techniques of assembly;
- personnel organisation;
- site organisation and layout;
- project communications;
- operational control (resource management);
- availability of skills and resources.

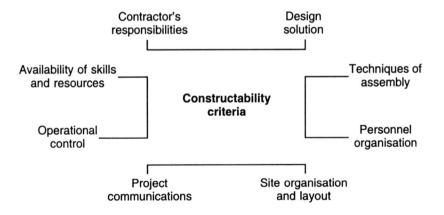

Figure 5.1   Constructability criteria to be considered during the construction phase

5.1   The contractor's responsibilities

Under a traditional contract (where the contractor is responsible only for construction), the contractor is responsible to the client's representative consultant, usually an architect or engineer, for 'all' activity on the construction site. Obviously, the contractor's stance will differ where an alternative form of procurement and contractual arrangement is adopted. For most construction projects, the construction or contracting organisation would select a site management team headed by a construction manager and/or engineer or a project and/or site agent who acts on behalf of the organisation at project site level.

To translate accurately the facets of design constructability to the workplace and to implement site constructability through effective and efficient organisation and management, construction management must seek to undertake and assume responsibility for the following:

- *Dialogue and negotiations with the client and the client's appointed consultants*   Constant liaison with the client and designer is essential if the translation of design constructability to the construction phase is to be effective. In addition, constructability must always be considered and implemented within the parameters, constraints and wishes of the client, so on-going dialogue must be fostered at the earliest opportunity. Certainly, design constructability has a much greater chance of success where the contractor has been consulted early in the total construction process – an advantage, of course, with, design–construct procurement.

- *Collation, checking and review of: drawings; design and construction details; specifications*   Constructability is vitally dependent upon the provision of good information and constant communication. The contractor must check that each drawing has been received, chase up where necessary, check that all drawings have the correct details, that all details are understood, that all details can be constructed, and liaise with the designer to ensure that the best constructability can be obtained from the design intention. If design rationalisation has been used in developing the details, then it must be confirmed that the contractor is fully conversant with the requirements. It may be that the contractor can see a more appropriate way to construct the design detail; therefore, liaison is essential to getting the best constructability from a design.

- *Developing a programme for construction*   The contractor will invariably develop a plan of construction that differs from the designer's preconception; this is the reality of separated inputs and the focus of their self-interests. For the purpose of encouraging design constructability at the workplace, it is essential that the contractor liaises with the designer to see how best the construction work on site can practically incorporate the design intention. This is, of course, a problem of traditional contracting, and one which may be helped by considering an alternative method of procurement. In terms of site constructability, the contractor is free to conceptualise the production process in any way he wishes and, as discussed subsequently, the programme can incorporate a number of useful elements to encourage better constructability. Perhaps the most essential element in programme development is the aspect of communication. It is vital that the programme reflects both the design intention and contractor's site conceptualisation in a practical and simple format. The actual method adopted, whether a traditional wall chart or a computer program must convey information in a simple form and facilitate communication between senior management and the operative at the workplace. It is the contractor's responsibility to maintain a programme and progressing mechanism that not only fulfils the contractor's requirements but also interfaces with the other project teams.

- *Selecting construction method and sequence*   Method and sequence of construction are two vitally important aspects of improving design constructability and site constructability. Constructability is dependent upon:

    - translating the elemental design conceptualisation into construction tasks through selecting the most appropriate methods of construction or assembly;
    - managing the interface between these design elements and the construction operations involved to promote a high level of integration and smoothness.
    - Work and/or method study applications are, of course, significant in addressing the above. With regard to constructability, continuous evaluation of method and sequence is essential and, moreover, feedback is paramount if on-going learning, review and action are to predominate.

- *Procurement, delivery, storage and use of materials*   The contractor is charged with the responsibility for correct and appropriate storage of all materials and components delivered to site. Material management is an important aspect of site constructability. Research studies have shown that up to 5 per cent or more of construction materials are often wasted during a typical contract through poor handling and storage procedures, in addition to misuse and inappropriate applications. Good constructability on site may help to reduce the expense incurred by reducing wastage and developing better site handling procedures. A simple example of such constructability in materials handling and storage is the elimination or minimisation of multiple handling, an aspect that not only accounts for a high proportion of natural wastage but also impinges upon the flow of operations on site.

- *Construction plant and equipment management*   It has always been the case within the construction industry that as the cost of labour has become more expensive so the need for mechanisation has increased, first to increase productivity and second to reduce the overall cost. In addition, the complexity of modern construction projects is such that plant and equipment are simply a prerequisite to achieving the means to construct. Plant management is an essential aspect of good constructability, because the translation of design to construction on site is fundamentally dependent upon both labour and mechanisation, so that the use of both must be evaluated hand in hand when considering how to construct any design.

- *Site organisation*   Many of the areas outlined, as well as other aspects yet to be mentioned, are influenced by the site organisation adopted by the contractor. Many wide-ranging issues are encapsulated within this aspect. It is essential to record that the contractor is charged with the responsibility for efficient and effective site organisation, and the careful consideration of this aspect alone can bring many positive benefits to the overall constructability of the project. Good basic site organisation and layout using sound management procedures, provide a fundamental starting point for constructability in most projects, since temporary organisation and setup is one of the first activities on any project, that is, it can set the benchmark for constructability.

5.2   Design solution

It has been clearly established that designing for good constructability on site requires considerable knowledge, forethought and empathy for the construction phase. Many aspects of constructability will have been integrated into the project at the design stage through the use of design analysis or design rationalisation techniques; therefore, many aspects of constructability during the construction phase will have been predetermined. It has been stated that constructability during the construction phase comprises two elements: first, design constructability, where the contractor must translate the design concept into an effective operational method and sequence; and second, site constructability and the ability to organise and manage around the operational aspects. Design constructability is obviously predetermined to a great extent by the chosen design solution, and site constructability is in many ways similarly affected.

The principles of design constructability may suggest, for example:

- simplifying the design elements;
- reducing the number of operations;
- using the same construction sequence;
- standardisation;
- dimensional coordination.

Once these factors and others are incorporated into the design they inherently impinge upon the construction methods and sequence. Design constructability is therefore set in many ways. Site constructability and the ways in which the contractor gathers and develops his resources can be manipulated however. Striking the balance between these two aspects of constructability is the key to successful implementation on site during the construction phase.

A constructable project will, in reality, be achieved only when the designer consciously sets out to anticipate construction problems, and when the contractor consciously sets out to appreciate what the designer is seeking to achieve. It is, therefore, essential in any construction project for the designer and contractor to liaise at the earliest opportunity, whether the procurement is traditional or non-traditional, as only in this way will genuine rather than token benefits be achieved.

Once work commences on site, constant dialogue and teamwork are essential to evaluating the design solution. Where, for example, a simplified detail has been designed for respective elements this can be evaluated as work proceeds and a learning sequence developed. In this way some flexibility in design constructability may be achieved; it really depends upon the specific aspects of the work. Certainly, evaluation of method and sequence is essential because, for example, the contractor may see the work in a way that differs from the intention in the design and therefore not get the best constructability from the element concerned. Evaluation and improvement here will again perhaps allow some refinement in the design and improve constructability.

It is essential when appreciating the design solution that the elements and details as presented represent a proactive attempt to aid the method and flow of construction. Therefore, the contractor must appreciate design constructability as a positive attempt and not be under any illusion that simplification or standardisation means less challenging design or mere uniformity or blandness, for example. Understanding each other's perspectives here can assist in promoting the common aims that should underpin the strategy for constructability.

5.3   Techniques of assembly

Once the design solution is determined, the contractor is to some degree restricted in the choice of method of assembly which in turn influences the sequence of construction work on site and the management of resources. A number of aspects are within the manipulation of the contractor and should therefore be considered with site constructability in mind:

- construction innovation;
- mechanisation;
- prefabrication.

Modern construction projects can employ a greater range of techniques available to construct or assemble the constituent parts than has been available in the past. This confers greater flexibility at the technical design stage, when it allows the designer to design and specify projects with greater complexity and demands knowing that the contractor has the wherewithal to complete. Specialisation in design input has increased demands and requirements for the construction process too, as design has essentially shifted from traditional solutions to more elaborate construction with much greater complexity. Notwithstanding these increased demands, the contractor has at his disposal a wealth of sophisticated plant and equipment, and a range of technical and management skills with which to respond. The contractor must select the appropriate level of resource and match this to the careful selection of method and sequence in order to give himself the necessary degree of innovation and flexibility in approach.

Most contractors have a range of approaches that can be applied to any given situation; the key is in the appropriate selection of that approach at that time. Innovation is a characteristic that singles out the contractor who consciously strives to produce better constructability from those who do not. Constructability relies to a great extent upon the contractor analysing his approach and manipulating resources to suit; but moreover it requires the contractor to think just that little bit further and creatively refine or tweak the approach subtly to get just that little bit more from the construction technique. Certainly the increasing demand upon construction from modern design can be burdensome, but it must be perceived not as a burden but as a challenge to the contractor.

Without doubt, construction has shifted markedly from the labour intensity that was characteristic in the past towards ever greater levels of mechanisation. Certainly, the way in which construction patterns have altered, and today's market, have virtually dictated this change. Client preferences for speed of construction, quality of service and genuine value for money have shortened construction contracts to the point where the contractor has little choice but to adopt a mechanistic approach rather than labour oriented construction. The contractor's selection of plant and equipment will be crucial to the success of the method and sequence; thus the level of mechanisation adopted must be matched to innovation in order to produce the most constructable approach.

Levels of technical innovation and mechanisation have affected not only the on site aspects of construction but also off-site aspects. While some construction can only be produced *in situ*, a larger proportion of construction activity may be undertaken off site through prefabrication. In this way the contractor's role has changed somewhat towards that of a co-ordinating assembler. This approach presents a considerable propensity for design constructability, as it encourages many of its intrinsic attributes, such as simplification, repetition, modular co-ordination and dimensional standardisation. That said, however, prefabrication does present problems for constructability in that the management process on site is more complicated, since sequencing, compatibility and tolerances must be carefully co-ordinated.

Prefabrication also presents problems of co-ordination between the designer and those responsible for the construction or assembly phase. In a radical situation the designer could design for complete prefabrication and total site assembly, but any error, misjudgement or lack of information by the design team would, in this case, have catastrophic effects on the construction phase. The designer therefore, is charged with incorporating all elements of design constructability that are desirable, namely, simplification, standardisation, repetition, modular and dimensional co-ordination, but he must allow also for an element of real construction input by the contractor in such a way that the contractor never loses control of 'construction' to 'assembly'.

5.4   Personnel organisation

Site personnel organisation

The actual form of personnel organisation on a construction project is, to all intents and purposes, determined by the nature and size of the contracting organisation and the particular type of building, construction or engineering contract being undertaken. It is also influenced, of course, by a number of well-recognised and commonly accepted principles of good personnel organisation.

The overriding principle is that there must be a clearly defined hierarchy of authority and responsibility, such that everyone on site knows their role, duties and responsibilities and to whom they are accountable and for whom they are responsible. This basic hierarchy is essential for establishing not only the chain of command but for fostering motivation, leadership, communication and feedback, all essential aspects of good site personnel organisation and, moreover, essential for the implementation of constructability. The hierarchical framework will assist greatly in developing dialogue and close co-operation between management and the various craft and general operatives working for the contracting organisation; it should also encourage a better working relationship between the teams of the various contractual parties, since communication routes are specific and known to all. Effective site personnel organisation is vital to the general smooth and efficient running of the site, and it commences before the contractor ever sets foot on site with the personnel selection for the project.

The implementation of good constructability practices does not in itself demand additional technical skills and abilities from the workforce. Rather, the requirement is perhaps to see the work tasks in a slightly different light. Personnel selection for constructability does not, therefore, demand more than the usual practice of selecting the currently available and appropriate staff and operatives for the job at the time. That said, the contractor should, where possible, select staff who are both conversant with the concept and tasks of constructability and more disposed to its implementation, because, as already noted, constructability does demand active communication and feedback, together with the readiness to learn as the project goes on and to implement the lessons learnt. Constructability does require flexibility of thinking in both management and the workforce.

Personnel organisation for constructability

The implementation of constructability is yet another onerous task that the site manager must address among all the other pressing matters of day-to-day site management. In the same way that in recent years quality management has developed into a specific managerial concept in its own right, so too could constructability. In an ideal situation, one member of the site management team can be charged with the duty and responsibility to oversee all aspects of constructability on site, whether it is transferring the principles of design constructability into practice at the workplace or implementing constructability across general site practices. In reality, however, the picture is not quite as simple. It is more likely that the busy site manager (or site agent) is asked to fulfil this role in addition to all other daily duties. This, of course, means that constructability may not receive the just and careful attention it deserves if its potential is to be maximised. Again, this is perhaps an issue of mentality and understanding on behalf of the contractor. The contractor who does take constructability seriously will no doubt reap the rewards. Case study material highlights a number of significant aspects within the remit of site personnel organisation for constructability. These are:

- client–contractor relationship at site level;
- personnel organisation structure;
- managerial style adopted by the site manager;
- labour resource size within the command of the site manager;
- supervisory style adopted by the manager with the workforce.

It will be seen in the cases presented later that particular ways of approaching and implementing the aforementioned aspects can bring positive results in the pursuit of better constructability on site.

Organisational charts

The site organisation chart sets the basis for site organisation structure, management and activity. Obviously, each organisation will adopt its own best structure according to its needs and activities, so a single approach is by no means applicable to all organisations. Some general principles of organisation charting may be stated, however. First, as site organisation becomes larger and more complex, each function tends to become a specialist activity. This lends itself usefully to constructability. On the smaller construction project a site agent may well assume responsibility for constructability as just another routine task, whereas on the larger project constructability may well become one of the specialist functions. Second, as activity becomes more specialist, so the control function must be better designed to ensure that the activity meets the planned requirements. The development of the control medium lends itself well to the linked development of communication and feedback routes, which again are aspects vital to the implementation of constructability.

Figure 5.2 illustrates the organisational structure necessary in the larger site organisation to pursue the potential for good constructability.

Within the site organisation, the assigned constructability manager or site agent assuming the duties for constructability should be responsible for:

- evolving a site structure that clearly defines the lines of authority, communication and feedback;
- structuring a clearly defined route for the communication of constructability to all interested parties in the project team;
- structuring clearly defined feedback routes for aspects of constructability from the workplace to management;
- on larger projects an assigned individual should be charged with the implementation of constructability at site level (in all its aspects);
- structuring a route for the feedback of the practice of constructability to the design team/consultants for on-going review; similarly, and also one for feedback to head office organisation for internal analysis and reviews.

5.5 Site organisation and layout

Research has shown that sound ergonomic site organisation and layout are prerequisites for achieving better constructability on site. Site constructability encapsulates those organisational and managerial attributes that influence on site activity, they focus on good basic site construction practice. These practices invariably evolve right from the initial setting up of the site.

Evaluation of the design and determination of construction method, operation and sequence by the contractor requires site management to

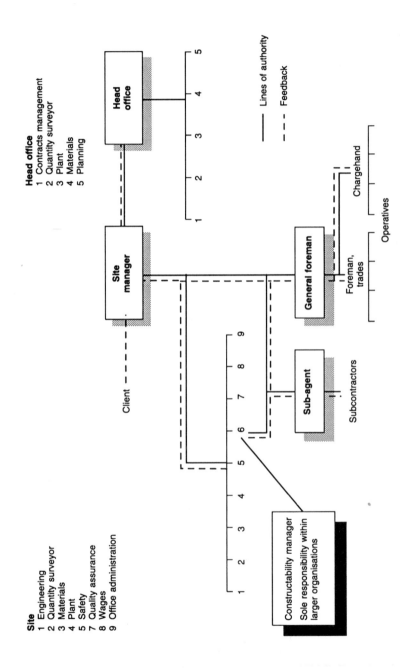

Site
1 Engineering
2 Quantity surveyor
3 Materials
4 Plant
5 Safety
7 Quality assurance
8 Wages
9 Office administration

Head office
1 Contracts management
2 Quantity surveyor
3 Plant
4 Materials
5 Planning

Head office

Site manager

General foreman

Sub-agent

Client

Subcontractors

Foreman, trades

Operatives

Chargehand

Constructability manager
Sole responsibility within larger organisations

——— Lines of authority
– – – Feedback

Figure 5.2   Position of the constructability manager within the organisation

analyse and review the construction demands in relation to the following aspects of site organisation and layout:

- access and traffic control;
- storage of materials;
- temporary facilities, services and temporary works;
- delineation of the site;
- safety;
- security;
- communication and control across the site;
- choice and siting of construction plant, tools and other equipment.

Access and traffic control

There is little doubt that constructability can be enhanced if access is well thought out. Efficient access for both materials and personnel is essential, as is efficient exiting from the site.

Site constructability is affected by the need for traffic control in two principal ways:

- to bring onto the site labour, plant and materials, to off- load, handle and store materials and equipment, and to deliver materials, components and plant to the workplace as work proceeds;
- to remove surplus excavated materials and debris, and to move plant and equipment off site when finished with;

The main points to be considered are:

- how items will be brought onto site;
- how items will be removed off site;
- how the design solution, construction method and sequences affect the two aforementioned criteria.

On the basis of these three aspects, site organisation decisions affecting access can then be made, the main areas of these being:

- the routing of traffic on and off site, and the potential dangers of merging with the public highway with its traffic flows and pedestrian movement;
- if the construction involves excavation on site, whether this will this require special provision, i.e. temporary roadways, spoil heaps, ramps, guardrails, etc.;
- if roads are part of the contract, whether these should be used as temporary road surfaces for construction traffic or whether other surfaces are a necessity;
- what checkpoints, signals and signposting are necessary to control traffic both on site and exiting from it.

Storage of materials

It is frequently said that a 'neat and tidy site is an efficient and well-run site'. Unfortunately, the practicalities of daily construction means that many sites are generally untidy. In reality, an untidy site is an inefficient site and will undoubtedly lose time and money. Storage is an aspect of site organisation and layout that can have severe consequences upon constructability. Storage may be broadly classified in the following categories:

- bulk materials;
- general materials;
- manufactured components;
- small fittings and components.

The essential aspects to consider in connection with constructability are:

- reduction of multiple handling of materials;
- protection of materials from damage by the weather;
- prevention of damage either to materials or to finished work by nearby production and/or through general carelessness;
- prevention of damages and loss resulting from handling and stacking materials during delivery, storage and movement around the site.

Constructability requires site management to give careful thought to the location of materials and components in relation to their assembled position in the works. Reducing the distances that materials must be transported will be reflected not only in better constructability but also in reduced production time and costs.

Temporary facilities, services and temporary works

It is no secret that both the physical conditions naturally prevalent on construction sites and the typical temporary facilities provided on many projects are generally quite bad. In addition, it may be said that on many sites only the barest facilities required by regulations are provided, if indeed any at all. The severely detrimental implication of this is often reflected in the attitude and morale of the workforce. As site staff spend long periods in temporary office accommodation and the workforce relies upon adequate facilities when not actually working on site, it is important that the contractor provides appropriate temporary facilities to meet all their needs. Not only is this provision a moral consideration: it is governed by legislation and must be taken seriously. In addition, as site constructability is dependent upon the efforts of both staff and workforce, maintaining a contented and stable project team should be paramount.

Delineation of the site

It will be seen subsequently that the delineation of the site both in terms of the overall confines and its division into work areas is important to constructability. Resourcing multiple workplaces is one of the daily tasks of the site manager. The ability to maintain co-ordination and control of these workplaces, and to communicate to them, is essential. Obviously, the physical nature and size of the site, together with the scope of the works to be undertaken determine the way in which it is organised and managed. Later, it will be seen that location, in addition to size and nature, is also influential to constructability.

Essentially, the contractor is often obliged to define the site with the use of fences and hoardings. This may follow conditions specified by the client or be demanded by legislation. For example, the type, height and construction of hoardings and fences where pedestrians must be protected and where entrances and/or exits are situated are all likely to be specified to the contractor.

The way in which the contractor divides up the site into specific production zones is however, at his own discretion. In practice, this will be determined by the his experience on former sites, although work and/or method study may help in determining ergonomic efficiency.

Safety

Like with any other aspect of construction, principles and practices of constructability must be implemented within the requirements for project safety. Safety has an influence upon site constructability, primarily because site safety procedures have a direct effect upon work methods and productivity. While there is considerable legislation governing site safety procedures, the wellbeing of both the staff and the workforce is reliant upon the proactive support of management. It is the responsibility of the site agent to ensure that a site is safe, that staff and workforce are adequately protected, educated and advised, and that the organisation's safety policy is rigorously implemented.

Security

In the same way that the contractor is responsible for site safety, the contractor is also charged with providing adequate site security. The provision of suitable hoardings and fences will, as previously mentioned, contribute to making a site well defined for the benefit of persons both on and off site. Expenditure in site security, whether this consists of secure areas, a watchman or lighting, is likely to be far less than that needed to pay for replacements for materials and equipment lost because of ineffective security. The inconvenience of waiting while lost materials and plant are replaced is likely to cost even more in terms of progress, so security is an important aspect of good site constructability.

Irrespective of the situation, three principles are crucial to security, namely that:

- No unauthorised persons should ever be allowed on to the construction site.
- All visitors should first report to the contractor's office and always be accompanied on or around the site.
- Any subcontractors and suppliers must abide by the contractor's arrangements as stated above.

Communication and control across the site

The location, extent and nature of a construction site directly determine the requirements for communication and control, both of which are critical to good constructability on site. It is somewhat obvious that the best lines of communication and control are those which are short and direct, (an aspect reviewed later in case study analysis) and while smaller sites may not require anything more than direct contact between the site agent and each member of the workforce, on a larger site with a bigger workforce the issue of communication and control can be problematic, and will demand the delegation of responsibility from the site manager to other heads of sections.

It is essential for the site manager to ensure that all heads of sections or departments on site, who are responsible for specific activities and functions are adequately briefed. Delegation and spans of control must be clearly defined, routes for communication and feedback established, and command and control mechanisms developed to ensure that all important aspects of production are covered. The various mechanisms for communication are explored in section 5.6 (p. 121).

Operational construction control is also discussed elsewhere (see section 5.7, p. 122). However, a number of other aspects of site control are essential to promoting better constructability. These include the following:

- *Material delivered to site*   Provision must be made to ensure that all materials are inspected and checked upon delivery to ensure that they meet with the specification required.
- *Components delivered to site*   These must be checked to ensure that they meet the specification required, are of the correct size, and have been made to the levels of quality demanded in the contract.
- *Materials and components produced on site*   Some on site works will be influenced by the technological and production requirements, such as for example a concrete batching plant. Mechanisms must be introduced to ensure that such materials and components meet the required specifications and qualities.

- *Quality and workmanship*   The contractor is responsible for ensuring that the works meet the quality required of the finished product. On site quality control procedures are therefore essential to good constructability.

Choice and siting of construction plant, tools and other equipment

Generally, the primary influence upon the choice of construction plant is the relationship between the design solution and the availability of mechanisation on the project. Site management must:

- determine the type of plant required in terms of function, method, reach, size, power and the like;
- determine if its use in the works will enable the expected method and outputs to be achieved with maximum efficacy.

The choice of plant and equipment for the undertaking of construction operations and sequence will obviously affect the requirement of site layout and organisation. For example a deep-basement construction will need larger excavators and these will require considerable areas for manoeuvring, while lorries will need clear access. High-rise construction will require space for cranes, etc.

5.6   Project communications

Communication and project information are the essence of constructability during the construction phase. Without effective communication between the contractual parties, and without accurate and reliable project information constructability has little chance of realisation and the project little chance of success. Moreover, one does not have to look beyond the aspects of communication and information to realise where the major problems of modern construction, like construction in the past, occurs.

Within construction the main method of communication of the client's requirements is the brief, the designer's intention by specification and drawings and the contractor's instructions by working drawings. Deficiencies of any kind in any location can place the project in jeopardy. Furthermore, methods of relaying information around the system and between the parties are essentially verbal, backed up by written communication where this is done. Research studies conducted in the UK[4-8] have shown quite unequivocally that communication and information lie at the root of many of the problems typically experienced within construction.

The main problems can be summarised as follows:

- inadequate client's brief;
- lack of documentation at the appropriate time;
- ambiguous design detailing;
- omissions and errors in the working drawings;
- variations and amendments to working drawings;
- misunderstanding of requirements by the contractor;
- lack of continuing dialogue throughout the project.

Problems can occur throughout the total construction process. Basically, the problems result from insufficient interaction between the parties. For example, developing the project brief is an interactive process between the client and the designer. Design formulation and design detailing is another interactive process where the designer must liaise closely with the client, and with other consultants and the contractor, to produce a practical and constructable design. Continuous appraisal and reappraisal must be sought to eradicate errors and omissions in the drawings, to see that each is suitable, communicable, accurate, dimensioned and referenced. Design constructability is dependent upon such a level of information and communication.

Site constructability is also dependent upon open information and communication. Variations and amendments will occur to drawings, specifications and other contract documentation, and the means of information flow must accommodate them. Misunderstandings may occur with a contractor who does not readily appreciate the implications of design, or who has not received adequate information be able to form a workable conclusion. Such aspects are essentially barriers to effective design and site constructability, and which can only be alleviated through open communication.

5.7   Operational control

Site constructability is fundamentally dependent upon sound principles and practices of operational construction control. Operational control encapsulates each and every aspect of day-to-day site management, within which activity can be broadly categorised as follows:

- general and specific operational control at site management and senior management (head office) levels;
- planning, progressing and controlling the works in relation to the main project variables (time, cost, quality);
- control of construction resources (labour, plant and materials).

Constructability is an obligation of each and every member of the project team, both staff and workforce, but the formal responsibility for constructability at site level rests with the site manager. The site manager is also responsible for operational or construction control, and therefore the project team manager is in the best possible position among to ensure that constructability is given a fair chance to succeed.

Pre-contract evaluation meeting

General construction control evolves before work commences on site. Once the contractor has tendered successfully, the first task of general control should be to arrange a pre-contract site meeting of all staff who have been involved with the preparation of the contract up to that stage with those who will have an involvement once work commences on site. This meeting is essential to co-ordinate the activities and participants and to get the project off to the best start and, moreover, it is an invaluable initial opportunity for the project team to evaluate constructability in detail prior to work on site. At this stage construction implementation of the design can be analysed, problems identified, and actions considered, and the opportunity created to resolve difficulties before they may become catastrophic. As a result of pre-contract evaluation, those participants responsible for specific aspects of site activity will be fully briefed and furthermore will appreciate the demands of constructability impinging upon their work.

Commencement meeting

It was noted earlier (p. 121) that communication of constructability concepts to the workforce is vital if the implementation of constructability is to be understood and accepted across all aspects of the project. Without this, any overall tangible benefit is likelt to be diminished. To assist understanding and acceptance, it is essential for senior management, through the site manager, to brief all members of the project team, staff as well as workforce. An effective medium for this is a project commencement meeting, which could be both informative and instructive and also present an opportunity for any member of the project team to raise any queries, and indeed to voice any fears that might be held. Only if everyone works towards better constructability will constructability be realised.

Site (control) meetings

During the contract as work proceeds on site, the most effective mechanism for control and the most appropriate instrument through which to review constructability continuously is the site meeting. Traditionally, such meetings, usually constituted as architect's or resident engineer's site meetings, are held monthly and involve everyone concerned with the contract.

Constructability is inextricably intermingled with this control mechanism, because site meetings normally assess and review the following:

- progress of the works, with reference to the main construction programme;
- cost of the work with reference to project budgets and cash flow forecasts and the extent, if any, of variations to the works and their effect on programme and cost;
- availability of resources with regard not to only the contractor's situation but also to those of any subcontractors involved;
- availability of design information in the form of drawings, details and specifications.

Where constructability forms a more formal aspect of project development, there is no reason why it should not merit a specific report and assessment at each monthly meeting, in addition to the four items listed.

Planning and progress

For effective construction control it is absolutely essential for management to know what has been achieved in relation to the project plan. Initially, the master (long-term) construction programme will present an overview of the project, but this is somewhat insufficient for the purposes of assessing constructability. As constructability demands communication, feedback and action on a continuous basis, short-term planning and progressing techniques are more applicable. Short-term planning is particularly pertinent, because it can be evolved around the monthly site meetings, which are the main project review and reporting mechanisms.

Whereas senior off-site management is predominately concerned with two main aspects, namely the profitability of the project and the overall effectiveness of site management, constructability is essentially a management function at site level. Site management will obtain the information necessary for assessing constructability implementation in two main ways which, again, take in short-term planning and control. These are;

- *Evaluating optimum production*   In addition to determining time, cost and workmanship parameters for each section, the operations and sequence of the work, the evaluation of the design solution based upon analytical method and/or work study techniques, historic records and experience will determine the optimum production for the work tasks.
- *Measuring actual output*   The only reliable method of assessing output is to measure the work done. Again, in addition to measuring cost and time expended, assessment of constructability must become an on-going activity within operational construction control.

The actual progress, including constructability analysis, can be recorded on the short-term programme, either weekly or daily, and achievement assessed against the short-term plans. On this basis, the work can obviously be speeded up, slowed down or generally manipulated as required to meet any requirement of the project. With regular and accurate plotting of production, real analysis is possible. Constructability assessment in such a continuous way allows constructability to become an active consideration at each monthly site meeting, as previously discussed (p. 124), and allows its best facets to be exploited.

Reliable short-term planning, progressing and analysis

- sub-divides the long-term and medium term construction programmes into more manageable and understandable plans for use at site level;
- provides for a much more accurate assessment of time, cost and quality aspects;
- facilitates more appropriate allocation of supervisors and workforce to the work;
- allows for closer and continuous monitoring of the works;
- enables management to look ahead to see possible disruptions, delays and difficulties;
- accurately reviews the actual work in relation to the plan to provide the facility for action.

Also, in addition to these points, short-term analysis

- allows for the provision of constructability analysis through detailed work and/or method study;
- provides feedback on design constructability to the designer and client and feedback on site constructability to the contractor for accurate recording purposes and data for future projects.

Control of resources

Effective construction control demands a great deal of organisational and administrative ability on the part of the site management team, or the individual site manager. The appropriate level of labour, sufficient materials and suitable plant and equipment must all be available at the right time and in the right place. Resource management is the most fundamental aspect of daily site construction control. If management is to achieve its own basic project objectives, namely maximum profit, in a minimum construction time while doing a first-class job, then it is essential to answer three basic questions:

1. If account is taken of the balance of all circumstances and situational conditions, what is the optimum production and most constructable way of meeting the project demands?

2. In attempting the above, what was the actual output achieved in terms of labour and plant utilisation, and to what level was the work constructable?
3. In evaluating, what can be done to increase production and improve constructability?

Again, control of resources is an aspect best managed within short-term programming and addressed within the remit of the monthly site control meeting already mentioned (p. 124).

5.8   Availability of skills and labour resources

For a building, construction or engineering project to be successful, management must be efficient and effective. While the management of materials and machinery is invaluable to a project, perhaps the most vital aspect of site management is the management of people. Management of the human resource has characterised construction throughout its history, since its origins in the labour-intensive activity of highly skilled and highly regarded craftsmen. Today, however, there can be little doubt that traditional skills are gradually being replaced by multiple, semi-skilled inputs, with mechanisation playing an ever more significant part. It is not simply that greater complexity in our buildings and structures demands greater mechanisation, although this is true, but in particular that patterns of work have changed with the introduction of new procurement systems and procedures for employment.

For example, labour-only subcontracting has replaced traditional waged labour to the extent that the main contractor is virtually a project co-ordinator, with all sections of the work carried out by specialists, an approach practised for many years in some countries.

Availability is an issue which affects the employment of both project staff and the site workforce. Difficulties in staffing can have a profound effect upon constructability.

Staff

It is often difficult to recruit and retain site management staff of the right calibre and with the right attitudes and knowledge to implement the best constructability practices. All construction suffers from the problems of mobility among its staff and workforce. It is well recognised that this aspect has always been especially difficult where mature and experienced staff are concerned, and a problem confronting particularly the larger contracting organisation. Although the industry shows signs of considerable fluctuation is this respect, there has in recent years been a tendency for larger contracting organisations to rationalise and centralise their business activities while construction activity is somewhat decentralised into geographic locations so as to limit the degree of mobility that they expect of their staff and workforce.

Workforce

Within the larger contracting organisation, the same problem exists in the workforce as does with its staff: the provision of work continuity. The problem is greater with the workforce because projects are in themselves itinerant in nature, requiring different trades and skills at specific times over the duration of the project. Certainly, the pursuit of good constructability can make matters worse to some extent, as it seeks to break down the complexity of trade interfaces, eliminate repeated visits to the workplace and generally rationalise the activity of the workforce into more efficient and effective but also smaller work packages. Staffing this approach can produce many logistic problems for a contractor used to progressing the work in the traditional manner.

Design for availability

It was stated in Chapter 4 that designers must design for the skills available, in fact, this was one of the principles for good buildability highlighted by a number of studies. Obviously, the designer cannot design for the explicit skills of a particular workforce, because that would be an ideal case, but in general he must anticipate the levels of skill likely to be available within a modern contracting organisation's workforce, and design within their capabilities. This is highly significant, because in the past a designer could design to great knowledge and bespoke skill levels within the general workforce, whereas sadly, today he must design for a diminished level of ability.

The contractor must, in appreciating the design details at tender stage, decide what resources are available and how their experience, skill and knowledge will best meet the design intention. If the designer has designed carefully and the contractor has selected his human resources wisely then the two aspects should be compatible. Any shortfall by the designer or the contractor behalf means that constructability may not be realised, and that problems will surface as work proceeds.

Maintaining resource levels

We have already discussed the difficulty of recruiting staff and operatives with the necessary skills and attributes to promote constructability through their activities on site; equally difficult is the retention of skilled inputs. The result of not thinking forward within the project to assure continuity of skilled input, can have catastrophic effects on the achievement of constructability. In practice, means the site agent must select his initial workforce carefully, liaising with other sites to maintain a continual flow of work and maintaining good relations with unions and labour offices to minimise the difficulties involved with the generally high turnover rates experienced within the industry.

Constructability and available skills

Within the aspect of availability of skills and labour resources, site management must

- assess carefully the constructability requirements demanded by the designer;
- select appropriately qualified, knowledgeable and skilled resources to meet the demands of design;
- maintain a small number of key staff and operatives to from the nucleus of the site team around which other resources can be varied;
- keep in contact with head office and other sites to level resources across projects when required;
- where staff and operatives of the right calibre are unavailable, give training to educate the project team in the principles and practices of constructability.

5.9   Constructability case study examples in the construction phase

This section presents a range of case study examples to illustrate the constructability concepts presented previously in this chapter. Examples are drawn from case studies in the management of building and engineering projects. Each example highlights particular aspects of the management of the works to improve constructability during the construction phase.

A large three-storey steel-framed building

This case study example focuses on 'simplification', a principle of design constructability, and a number of site constructability aspects: site organisation; trade sequencing; and plant and equipment management to enhance constructability in the construction phase.

The project comprised a new building to a well-established development consisting of a lightweight steel portal frame with hi-tech cladding enclosure built on piled pad and beam foundations and incorporating an extensive traditional brick-block office compartment to one elevation. Construction operations were managed such that there was a particularly smooth flow of work from one end of the office section to the other, incorporating an almost continuous sequence of trades, while the frame was assembled as a completely free-standing element in parallel. Although similar projects undertaken locally had utilised a tower crane, this project sequenced the use of a mobile crane, which while easily providing for all the site demands, was much more economic in operational time and cost. Further constructability examples on the same project saw the simplified construction of the foundation details, which, while incorporating a pile, pad and ground beam design, were designed explicitly for minimising the below-ground construction time. Review of the task duration for this aspect showed a saving of over 20 per cent in man-hours in comparison with similar work undertaken on other projects on the development.

Groundworks for water treatment plant

This case study example emphasises the importance of simplicity and trade sequencing for improved constructability in the planning of groundworks for installations within a water treatment plant.

The example describes the setting out detail and casting sequence for the reinforced *in situ* concrete slabs of two ponds within the water treatment plant. Constructability consideration focused upon the best arrangement of bays for casting the slab. Essentially the groundworks for each pond consisted of a $2\,200$-m^2, 250-mm-thick reinforced concrete slab with downstand edge beam. The perimeter of the slab had a 150-mm upstand, this being the starter for the 200-mm-wide pond walls, 1.75 m high. The finished ponds were finished to their internal surfaces with water-retaining butyl lining.

Figure 5.3 shows the setting-out and casting sequence devised by the contractor. The slab was divided into twelve bays, each approximately 6 m wide and 30 m long. Casting alternately between the two ponds on successive days, two bays on each pond could be cast, one each morning and one each afternoon, over a fourteen day period. To assist this undertaking, a mechanical power-float was used on each bay and this was shown to speed up the overall casting process while finishing the concrete in a single operation to an acceptable standard to receive the lining material.

Concrete pipe rack bases for petrochemical pipelines

This case study example reviews an innovative approach to improving constructability in the prefabrication and installation of concrete pipe rack bases for extensive petrochemical pipelines within large petrochemical processing facilities.

The works involved the prefabrication and installation of an ongoing series of concrete pipe rack bases. The contractor, employed under a three year term contract, had worked in close association with the in-house engineering design team of the client, a large organisation in the petrochemical industry. It was therefore commonplace for the design and engineering works super-

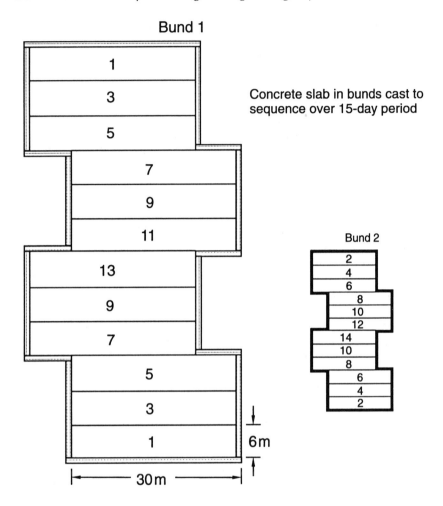

Figure 5.3   Illustration of the casting sequence to water treatment bund slabs

intendent to liaise with the contractor's site manager and site engineer with a view to determining improved constructability in many aspects of the site works.

The consideration of constructability in this example focused upon the techniques of prefabrication and installation of concrete bases. Historically, the client procured rectangular 2.0 m × 1.5 m × 0.75 m pre-cast concrete units incorporating four 20-mm-diameter bolts set in jigs. The bases, cast in the contractor's site compound, were transported to the pipe trench on a flat trailer and handled by a small mobile crane hired when required for this purpose.

An alternative pipe base design was proposed by the client's works super-intendent which improved the site constructability characteristics of the works considerably. A 2.4 m × 1.2 m × 0.60 m splayed pre-cast concrete pipe rack base was designed with only two 25-mm-diameter bolts jigs, these being quite sufficient to locate and secure the pipe that it supported. This alternative design while taking approximately the same length of time to fabricate, cost 15 per cent less to produce. In addition, an innovative aspect was that, as the bases were cast, strap handles were fixed such that the completed units could be handled by a lorry mounted handling crane and transported to the pipe trench, also to be off-loaded and located in position by the crane with the aid of the extendable boom. The client recorded an approximately 20 per cent saving in the cost of procurement of the same and similar pipe bases over the course of the term contract.

Cranage for multi-storey tower blocks

This example reviews the utilisation of cranage in the construction of two multi-storey tower blocks procured under a design–construct contract. It highlights the importance of constructing for optimum use of resources and maximum accessibility in promoting improved constructability.

Figure 5.4 illustrates two options considered for providing the necessary cranage to the construction of the two tower blocks. In the first option, it was considered that the stanchion of the tower crane could be built in as part of the building's structural frame, with two tower cranes being used, one for each block. However, the design–construct contractor ultimately adopted a free-standing external tower crane to service the two tower blocks simulta-neously. Moreover, there was sufficient access and working space on the site to effect the dismantling of the crane towards project completion. This determined a direct saving on cranage costs of approximately 30 per cent and, in addition, the contractor had use of the tower crane on subsequent construction projects, a contributed saving in real terms of a further 35 to 40 per cent.

Installing precast concrete run-off channelling within a chemical engineering plant

This case study example considers the installation of large precast concrete duct channels within a chemical engineering plant building, where access was restricted and the environment hostile to manual work. It illustrates the consideration of constructability for co-ordination, tolerances, simplicity in site operations and innovative assembly techniques.

The contractor, employed under an on-going term contract, was asked by the client to work with the client's in-house design–engineering unit to

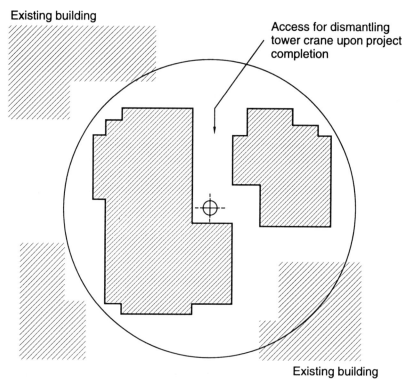

Figure 5.4   Positioning of cranage for constructing two multi-storey tower blocks

determine the most appropriate method for installing a number of wash-down–run-off ducts totalling around 1000 m in length. These were to be constructed within two process plant buildings whose access was limited and environment unfavourable, and would thus make traditional *in situ* construction problematic. The solution developed by the contractor and the client's in-house design–engineering unit was to prefabricate the duct in pre-cast concrete and use a rather innovative method of installation.

Figure 5.5 illustrates the design and construction features of the pre-cast duct. To prepare the existing floor slab for the duct installation, chases were cut into the slab, the concrete broken out and the remaining depth of sub-floor material excavated. 30 mm was allowed on the trench bottom and faces for working tolerances when the pre-cast units were positioned. These were bedded in lean-mix blinding to locate the duct channels in the trench and ensure the necessary falls.

The innovative aspect to the work was that the existing pulley-gantries within the plant were actually utilised to hoist and lower the pre-cast con-crete sections into position. This, in fact, enabled sections 3 m long to be

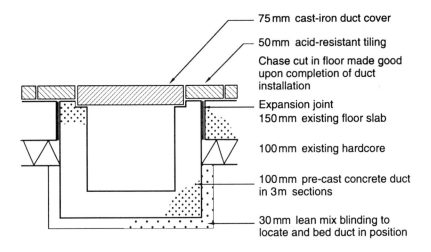

75 mm cast-iron duct cover

50 mm acid-resistant tiling

Chase cut in floor made good
upon completion of duct
installation

Expansion joint
150 mm existing floor slab

100 mm existing hardcore

100 mm pre-cast concrete duct
in 3 m sections

30 mm lean mix blinding to
locate and bed duct in position

Figure 5.5   Pre-cast concrete drainage channelling within a chemical process plant

handled and positioned whereas if this facility had not been available, the contractor had said, that only 750 mm or 1000 mm could have been used, owing to the restrictive working space for handling. The client's in-house design unit estimated that the novel approach to handling the pre-cast units together with the use of the larger pre-cast units themselves, reduced the cost by around 25 per cent. In addition, it obviated the need for the contractor's workforce to undertake many traditional casting operations in an unfavourable environment.

Internal finishes in a refurbishment project

This short case study example presents an illustration of the consideration of constructability to internal finishes during a refurbishment project. The work incorporated a single operation dry-lining detail to internal partitioning, a solution suggested by the contractor in preference to that originally specified. The external walls were lined with thermal insulation lining board applied in large sections to the inner leaf blockwork by plaster dabs. The party walls were lined with plasterboard with filled and taped joints. The non-loadbearing stud partitions were lined with foil-backed plasterboard, which enabled the lining to be fixed by the joiners without a dependency upon plasterwork trades. Eliminating the joinery – plasterwork interface, this simple operation was carried out wholly by the contractor and was shown to reduce the man hours spent by up to 30 per cent.

5.10   Constructability in the construction phase: summary, overview and strategies

Summary of construction criteria

In reviewing construction criteria for constructability, there is considerable evidence, to suggest the following:

- Two aspects are highly significant, these being:

  - design constructability – the transfer of design analytical aspects to the construction phase (i.e. buildability);
  - site constructability – the impact of organisation and management aspects to improve the contractor's work on-site.

- Among the many aspects which must be reviewed by the contractor in association with the two factors above, essential constructability considerations are encapsulated within eight broad groups:

  - the contractor's responsibilities;
  - design solution;
  - techniques of assembly;
  - personnel organisation;
  - site organisation and layout;
  - project communication;
  - operational control;
  - availability of skills and resources.

- Consideration has shown, quite unequivocally, that site practices are equally as important as design consideration in pursuing better constructability.
- Evidence from case study examples has indicated that considerable time and cost benefits can accrue from implementing some of the ideas suggested, some examples up to 30 per cent savings in time and up to 25 per cent savings in cost.
- Research has demonstrated that the potential for better constructability on-site is not free, in terms of time, cost or effort. Constructability is fundamentally dependent upon management influence, and this in turn is determined by developing the right attitude in the site-based team. Co-ordination, information and communication are also highlighted as essential to the organisation and management success of the project.

Constructability strategy during the construction phase

Questions

The contractor should ask the following questions:

- Does the construction team on site truly appreciate the construction implications of the design solution?
- Where constructability been incorporated into the design (design analysis) does the site team understand its orientation?
- How can the aspects of design constructability and site constructability be accommodated within the method, sequence and activities of construction?
- Has the contractor got the necessary resources (management, labour, plant and materials) to get the best constructability from the construction process?
- How is the contractor going to plan, monitor and control performance to achieve the best constructability?

Considerations

The contractor should seek to consider carefully and implement the following principles of good constructability during the construction phase:

- Construct for both design constructability and site constructability.
- Construct for available resources.
- Construct for simplicity in site operations.
- Construct for accessibility.
- Construct for simplified trade sequences.
- Construct for standardisation.
- Construct for co-ordination (dimensional and modular).
- Construct for accommodating innovation, change and variation.
- Construct with information flow and communication in mind.
- Construct with well-defined and limited workplaces.
- Construct for closer interaction with the designer and client, to meet design requirements and corporate objectives of the client.

Action

For the best possible constructability during the construction phase, the contractor should ensure that he

- appreciates the design constructability consciously detailed into the design for translation into activities on site;
- works in association with the designer to achieve the above;

- helps to co-ordinate the issue and flow of project information from design to construction;
- informs both staff and workforce of the demands placed upon them by project constructability;
- appoints a constructability manager (or constructability team) to oversee constructability as a managerial concept in its own right;
- applies site constructability in all its facets to make all activities on site more efficient and effective;
- monitors and controls constructability on site and takes action, where necessary, to manage problems and change;
- provides a constructability review of on-going aspects and reports (feedback) at site meetings;
- provides a positive attitude in leadership and motivation of staff and workforce to encourage better constructability on site;
- co-ordinates the technical and managerial content of all work sections (packages) to accommodate subcontract works with his approach;
- utilises specialist inputs to advise on specific problems of constructability or technical matters;
- analyses work continually to derive the most efficient and cost-effective alternatives in constructability.

In the procurement and design phases, the client and his professional advisers may consciously decide that they wish to pursue the concept of constructability to realise any benefits that they perceive. The ramifications of decisions made by them materialise for the contractor on site. Within the construction phase, however, the contractor has some choice in the level of commitment that he wishes to give to constructability; moreover, he can structure his own approach.

As has been explained in this chapter, site constructability, and to a large extent design constructability requires little more commitment than the implementation of good site practices. Benefits to the contractor accrue through sound organisation and site management, effective and efficient use of resources and improved communications, control and feedback. All of those facets of basic but good site practice undoubtedly lead to a more cost-effective construction phase with benefits not just to the contractor but to all contractual parties.

References

1. A. Griffith, 'Buildability: The Effect of Design and Management on Construction, A Case Study', SERC/Heriot-Watt University Publication, Edinburgh, 1985.
2. Construction Industry Research and Information Association (CIRIA), *Buildability: An Assessment* CIRIA Publications, London, 1983, Special Publication no. 26.

3. S. Adams, *Practical Buildability*, CIRIA/Butterworth, London, 1989.
4. Building Research Establishment (BRE), 'Failure Patterns and Implications', *BRE Digest*, 176, 1975.
5. National Economic Development Office (NEDO), *Achieving Quality on Building Sites*, NEDO, London, 1987.
6. A. Griffith, 'A Critical Investigation of Factors Influencing Buildability and Productivity', PhD Thesis, Heriot-Watt University, Edinburgh, 1984, unpublished.
7. F. P. McDermott, 'Buildability: Delays and Disruptions to Construction Sequence', SERC Report, 1986, unpublished.
8. O. Osman, 'The Modelling of Factors Influencing Observed Manpower ProductiveTime within the Site Production Process', PhD Thesis, Heriot-Watt University, Edinburgh, 1989, unpublished.

6 Constructability in Use

The preceding chapters have considered the contribution of constructability at various key stages in the total construction process where the contribution is clear and pronounced, in procurement, design and the construction phase. One does not necessarily think of the maintenance phase of the total construction process if one is considering constructability. This should not imply, however, that constructability has little or no part to play in the use and maintenance of the construction product, that would, in fact, be far from the truth. Constructability has a valid contribution to make in the operational strategy of a building or engineering project. This is clear to a major extent in, for example, the asset management of new capital projects and to a lesser but important extent in preventive and condition-based maintenance management to existing projects. Both of these aspects are, of course, highly significant to the client's level of satisfaction with the finished product and in the use and upkeep of that product. This chapter considers the potential of constructability in application to the use and maintenance of a building or engineering product in the light of increasing requirements for maximum utilisation, minimum down-times for maintenance and repair and the ever closer control of life cycle costs in today's high-cost construction assets.

6.1 Maintenance – a total process approach

Constructability in use and maintenance can be viewed succinctly in terms of the total construction process as follows:

- *procurement* the rationalisation of 'best-buy' procurement techniques, in considering the best overall management package, i.e. inception right through to eventual replacement;
- *design* consideration of design for ease of use, reliability, maintainability and lower life cycle costs;
- *construction* facilitating understanding of the physical properties of the building to obtain best operability and use;
- *Management systems* to introduce the optimum operating techniques, reduce down-time for repairs and maintenance and improve use and care of the built asset;
- *communication and feedback* support systems for use and maintenance activity are essential to effective monitoring and control and provide constructability feedback for future designs (both technological and financial).

Strategies for asset management are essentially dealing with two distinct categories of application, namely

- new assets;
- existing assets.

As mentioned earlier (p. 138), constructability can be influential in considering both new and existing assets but there is little doubt that its potential is greater in its application to new assets where constructability to reduce maintenance and repair can be introduced at the briefing and design stage.

Constructability in existing assets is obviously not concerned with the terotechnological approach to reduce maintenance requirements, but is concerned with the site constructability aspect, of carrying out the maintenance and refurbishment, i.e. it is essentially an ergonomic consideration.

New asset management

Constructability in, for example, project management, by definition requires an inception to completion philosophy and imparts great demands on the total construction process. Constructability in the asset management of new projects requires one to go further, in that total asset management demands an inception to replacement philosophy. The strategy for constructability in new asset management commences with pre-investment studies and continues through design, construction, and the life cycle in use. Constructability for effective maintenance must be foreseen at the earliest possible stage in this asset management process and the user requirements for maintenance and major repair need to be incorporated within the design and construction processes. Of course, there will be a trade-off in the decisions that must be made in respect of constructability. The question is: is it in fact more cost-effective to consider constructability in order to eliminate future maintenance requirements, or simply to undertake the maintenance when eventually it must occur?

Existing asset management

Strategies in the management of existing assets are concerned with activities directly within the maintenance and repair functions. Constructability is therefore also limited in this direction. The accent of constructability here is on considering the technological and managerial aspects of undertaking maintenance and repair, rather then attempting to alleviate it thorough consideration in the earlier stages of the building process. It therefore focuses upon the planning, monitoring and control of the ways in which maintenance and repairs are actually carried out, so that through meaningful considerations better methods can be developed. Constructability can form part of

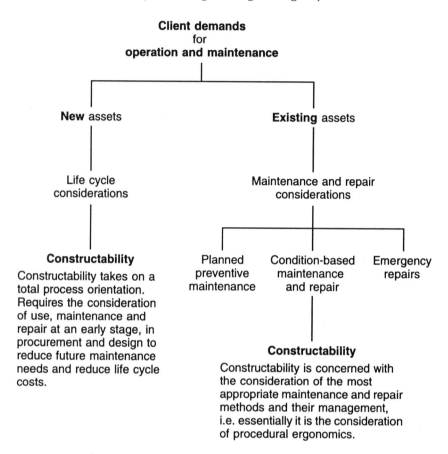

Figure 6.1   *Constructability in the operation and maintenance of building assets*

both a planned preventive maintenance strategy and a condition-survey-based maintenance-and-repair approach (see Figure 6.1).

Both of these aspects are essential to determining the cost of ownership of the client's future asset. Today's clients are concerned with the achievement of 'best-buy' economic costs across the total construction process, and this means that consideration must be given not only to the construction cycle but also to the costs of ownership and use (occupancy costs).

6.2   The requirements for maintenance and repair

The management requirements for maintenance and repair activities obviously consist of a sound knowledge of technology and the expertise to identify demands. Terotechnological considerations go beyond these basic prerequisites, requiring management to perceive the requirement for main- tenance and repair within the context of the preceding phases, i.e. procure- ment, design and construction.

Overall, the basic concepts of maintenance and repair management follow those principles utilised in any form of management, that is: setting aims and objectives; developing practices to achieve these aims and objec- tives; and considering action to rectify problems and difficulties in carrying out those practices, i.e. planning, monitoring and control.

The underlying principles of management for maintenance operations tend to remain the same, irrespective of the different applications. Require- ments differ, however, according to a wide range of factors, the primary ones being the type, size and characteristics of the building, structure or other works requiring the maintenance and repairs.

Maintenance and repair to small building works, for example, may be controlled satisfactorily on what might be considered to be an *ad hoc* basis, where the client simply employs a tradesperson on a jobbing works arrange- ment. Clients with more extensive requirements may, conversely, procure maintenance and repair on an ordered works or contract basis, following a condition survey as part of a phased maintenance strategy.

Constructability approach

A constructability approach to maintenance and repair strategy, involving life cycle cost consideration, imparts a more comprehensive approach to asset management but does, of course, involve a greater degree of organisation and management than the aforementioned approaches. It is most likely, although this is hard to quantify precisely, that such an approach will promote many positive benefits to maintenance and repair strategy, the most persuasive being the potential reduction in maintenance and repair costs. However, this potential is not achieved without cost itself. A constructability approach is heavily dependent upon the client and appointed consultants avidly wishing to pursue its objective, an increased requirement for management of the processes involved and constant monitoring, recording and appraisal for incorporation into future strategies. Even with goodwill and the best intent among a few, there is, in general, little appreciation of the issues involved, a short-term view of projects rather than a longer-term and perhaps more cost- effective view, and little information reliably recorded for analytical decision making by clients for future construction projects.

Constructability requires the client to consider the maintenance and repair characteristics of the building, structure or other work as his notional outline ideas of the project are developed from the brief into the design and subsequently through construction or assembly.

Designing out maintenance will, of course, not be uppermost in the minds of many designers and engineers, who are preoccupied with meeting what are considered to be overriding principles of construction time, quality and cost. Moreover, many designers will simply be out of touch with the operation, maintenance and repair functions, being ostensibly design-oriented, so any propensity to reduce maintenance, repair and occupancy costs is rarely envisaged. Designing out, procuring out and constructing out future maintenance and repair is always going to be a difficult concept to grasp not so much in rational as in quantifiable terms, and also it will always be a matter of compromise as to what is a cost-effective consideration and what is not. The point is that if constructability is taken seriously by the parties involved, in particular the client and his design and/or engineering consultant, then there is no reason why some of the more obvious aspects of constructability in maintenance and repair should not be considered. For example, a particular material or component with a known increased life span, if it meets the project criteria, costs the designer no more to specify and entails no more work than an inferior one. The old adage applies: the cost of applying a coat of paint is roughly the same, regardless of the paint's price and quality.

Key aspects of implementation

There are essentially two key aspects which the consideration of constructability can impart, namely:

- designing-in building and/or engineering elements with greater durability, reliability and longevity to effectively minimise future maintenance and repair and reduce overall life cycle costs;
- managing the operation and use of the finished product to retain optimum performance characteristics and support the above by considering constructability aspects of maintenance tasks and procedures.

6.3 Capital project management

As today's clients are seeking an overall best-buy option in the buildings that they procure, with greater emphasis on economic costs across the total building process, so constructability becomes ever more important. Taking on an almost terotechnological approach, constructability can form a fundamental and vital part of the life cycle development of a new construction or engineering project.

Life cycle stages

The ten various key stages in the life cycle of each capital project development may be summarised as follows:

- *conception* – notional formulation of the project concept by the client;
- *appraisal* – decision by client, financiers and consultants to progress to feasibility;
- *formulation* – detailed feasibility aspects of the project's worth;
- *evaluation* – extensive review of development options;
- *procurement* – selection of project framework, contract form, organisation and management approach;
- *design* – detailed concept development, including life cycle cost plan and consideration of value management;
- *construction* – on-site production phase;
- *completion, commissioning and handover* – client accepts responsibility for finished product;
- *operation and use* – performance proving under working conditions.
- *maintenance and repair* – general upkeep of the product under normal operating conditions.

The consideration of constructability for new capital project developments requires that thinking on constructability takes place in each of the ten key life cycle stages. It is considered somewhat axiomatic that the client must favour this approach, for the reasons already given, but if he is to achieve it, then one or more of the following must be ensured:

- that the client has sufficient in-house knowledge and expertise to consider maintainability of the finished product;
- that the design and/or engineering consultant appointed has the requisite knowledge of, and expertise in, the maintainability and operating costs of the finished product, and can consider these as the design is formulated;
- that a facilities, maintenance or asset manager is appointed as part of the consultant team to facilitate a long-term view of maintainability as the project is developed.

The involvement of a maintenance or asset manager in new project work is essential if effective maintenance and upkeep of the finished product is to be realised. Where, for example, the client has in-house expertise in maintenance and operation, then advisers should be available for consultation on new capital projects.

The implementation of constructability to meet the future needs of maintenance and operation requires the following contributions by the maintenance or asset manager:

- *formulation* – evaluation of the upkeep, maintenance, repair, and operational implications of the proposed development;
- *procurement* – assessment of the options for ensuring the effective operation and maintenance of the finished product;

- *design* – evaluation of documents, drawings and specifications with regard to operation and maintainance aspects;
- *construction* – monitoring of the future maintainability of the product throughout the production stage to ensure that criteria of workmanship and performance are met;
- *completion, commissioning and handover* – evaluation of the product with regard to performance and maintainability, consideration of product support for the installation, equipping, and development of a planned maintenance and upkeep programme;
- *operation, use, maintenance and repair (post-commissioning)* – monitoring, maintenance and upkeep programme and review.

Constructability objectives

In capital project management, constructability means essentially attempting to comply with the first of the two key constructability considerations specified (p. 142), namely the designing in of building and/or engineering elements with greater durability, reliability and longevity in order to minimise future maintenance and repair, meet the needs of occupancy and reduce overall life cycle costs. To achieve this objective, two things are essential, as follows:

- The necessary knowledge and expertise (either in-house or consultant) must be brought in at the earliest opportunity, and there must be constant dialogue between the maintenance consultant and the client and his design and/or engineering consultant.
- The requirements for future operations and life cycle costs must be accurately specified at the appropriate stages in the developmental processes and be effectively incorporated into the design drawings, specifications and contract documentation.

Dialogue with the client (user)

For a tangible contribution to be made to the ten key stages in the life cycle of new capital projects (p. 143) there must be constant liaison between the client, or prospective user, and the design team, including the maintenance and facilities management input. Through in-house or external consultants, advice must be sought on how design solutions are likely to affect the maintenance and operating costs. It is essential that persons with the appropriate expertise be brought in at the earliest opportunity to liaise with the client at the briefing, design and procurement stages. Only then can the design incorporate those elements, materials and components that will best promote longer-term durability and reliability, and in so doing reduce the likely future costs of maintenance and repair. This contribution relies heavily on the design leader being either conversant with, or advised by the maintenance specialist on, the use of new and technologically innovative materials. It also relies on the maintenance specialist being able to advise on the life cycle and essential costs of such materials. The absence of such advice is, of course, a major reason for designers not pursuing these issues with perhaps less vigour than they should.

Specification

With the early involvement of a maintenance and/or facilities management specialist in the developmental processes, on-going and valuable dialogue can be encouraged between the project participants, but this asset can never be realised if useful thoughts and ideas are not implemented within the formulation process. To achieve the objectives, this contribution must be incorporated into the project documentation and form a real part of the project requirements. Discussion at the briefing stage, and consultation between the design leader and the maintenance and/or facilities management specialist, must be followed by appropriate processes of specification. Specifications for design elements, and their subsequent construction or assembly operations, must seek to provide for greater reliability and longevity in the materials and components used, and more carefully conducted procedures to ensure that potential benefits are not compromised through poor workmanship practices.

Careful specification should consider the life span characteristics of materials and components, and incorporate these with the optimum, but balanced, characteristics from considered alternatives. It is essential that such maintainability criteria are specifically written-in to project documentation and not merely implied generally, since only if definite and measurable requirements are specified can they be accurately translated in the construction process.

Lifespan considerations

Determining the lifespan of the finished product or its components is an extremely complex process. Prediction is made all the harder by the knowledge that inadequacies in design and workmanship contribute considerably to deterioration. Even where constructability is designed and built in, on-site problems may nullify a potential benefit being realised.

Another constraint to the accurate assessment of component lifespan is the absence of detailed information to aid prediction. Although there is some historic data on traditional design, materials and components, information is generally lacking on broad building or engineering types and, even where some exists, the records are frequently insufficient to facilitate accurate assessments to be made.

In addition, predictions on lifespans and life cycles of components, where made, tend to focus on physical obsolescence; and while it is well appreciated that functional or technical obsolescence will be significant determinants over time, these aspects are difficult to calculate in the overall cost profile.

Various studies have addressed the problems of lifespan prediction, and some of these are included in the Select Bibliography (p. 182); the reader should consult them for further information. One fact that does emerge from empirical studies is that the lifespan of some design elements and components is easier to assess than others, and here considering constructability at the design stage can play a part in selecting those solutions, elements and components that demonstrate some propensity to increase durability and longevity and, in so doing, reduce the cost of maintenance and repair in the longer term.

6.4   Condition-based maintenance management

Condition-based maintenance and repair is work initiated as a result of the deteriorating condition of a component following routine inspection or *ad hoc* observation. As the concept relates to retrospective rather than pre-emptive maintenance constructability is concerned primarily with the procedures and practices employed in the work.

Three aspects of constructability consideration are applicable, namely to ensure the following:

- that condition survey procedures are effectively carried out;
- that the technological methods and managerial procedures used to undertake maintenance and repair are technically appropriate and cost-effective;
- that adequate records are maintained on the condition of the building or structure and that the remedial work undertaken promotes useful feedback for future projects.

Of these three aspects, the most important are undoubtedly the latter two.

Technological and managerial procedures

We saw earlier (Chapters 4 and 5) that constructability can influence these in two essential ways, as follows:

- Design constructability   The focus upon design analysis brings light to bear on such factors as simplification, rationalisation, co-ordination, and integration to improve constructability (Chapter 4).
- Site constructability   The focus upon good site practices directs attention towards effective organisational and managerial means of improving constructability (Chapter 5).

The impact of both these aspects and the action necessary to ensure their successful implementation, have already been considered in the chapters mentioned; the reader seeking further information at this point is therefore referred back to them.

Performance and performance information feedback

There is little doubt that many projects do not achieve the quality of finish and levels of performance expected by the design and/or engineering consultant, or, indeed, the client. In many cases, shortfalls in expected performance are a result of inadequacies in design, failing materials and components, poor workmanship and site management. Moreover, problems often result from combinations of these aspects and are therefore difficult to diagnose and relate to a specific cause. Performance problems can be quite small and simple, or extensive and complex; but, irrespective of their nature, they all result in increased user costs and are therefore an important issue to the client and the occupier.

Many of the problems witnessed in the construction industry go unchanged simply because there is often little done to monitor and record accurately what problems have occurred, what remedial action has been taken and how much this has cost.

The importance of operation, maintenance and repair feedback cannot be over-emphasised. While it is not really a factor of constructability *per se*, it is essential to the overall objective of providing the client with best buy procurement. Certainly, where constructability is avidly pursued from the project's outset, an ancillary activity must be to formulate a procedure for monitoring and recording performance data to provide feedback on the cost–benefit implications of constructability itself.

One body of opinion holds that the strict financial limits for capital cost frequently placed on today's construction projects can result only in poor performance. It is more likely, however, that problems occur because clients pay less attention to operation and maintenance aspects at the briefing and design stages, and do not encourage the follow-through of maintenance considerations. In such cases, there is little likelihood of any feedback being obtained on the use and performance of the product, and therefore little information available for assessing future projects.

6.5   Constructability in use: summary, overview and strategies

Summary of operation and maintenance

In reviewing the consideration of constructability with regard to operation and maintenance, the following major points emerge:

- For constructability to play a significant part, it must be thought of as a total project concept, concerned with all stages of the construction and/ or engineering process and involving a life cycle cost approach.
- A distinctly different consideration of constructability is needed for

  - new assets, which require a capital project approach with life cycle orientations, and
  - Existing assets, where an ergonomic approach to maintenance, repair and refurbishment is appropriate following a condition-based survey

- Constructability in capital project management relies upon the careful consideration of life cycle cost implications within the following ten stages of the development process:

  - conception;
  - approval;
  - formulation;
  - evaluation;
  - procurement;
  - design;
  - construction;
  - completion, commissioning and handover;
  - operation and use;
  - maintenance and repair;

- Successful constructability during the user phase relies heavily upon:

  - the client having in-house knowledge and expertise;
  - that failing this, a design consultant being able to consider maintainability within the design;
  - a specialist maintenance and/or facilities manager being brought into the development team, early enough to impart a useful contribution.

- Successful implementation is dependent upon the following:

  - on-going dialogue being maintained between the maintenance specialist and the client and/or consultants.
  - requirements being carefully and accurately specified in project documentation;
  - production of maintenance manuals, with some explanation of their main components.

- In both new capital projects and existing buildings or structures the performance should be carefully monitored, and accurate records of procedures and cost of maintenance, repair and use obtained to provide feedback for future projects.

Constructability strategy for operation and maintenance

Questions

The client must at the project conception stage ask himself the following questions:

- Is the focus on the total life cost, or merely on the capital construction cost of the project?
- What is the likely performance of the building asset over time, i.e. what are the expected lifespans of the component parts?
- What is the life cycle cost of the product and its parts?
- Is there awareness of the implications of not considering maintenance and repair early in the project, i.e. the future effect of maintenance and repair on use and costs?
- Is sufficient information available on life cycle aspects, maintenance, repair and operation to incorporate into the project development?
- Has the client got the necessary in-house knowledge and expertise to answer these questions, or must specialists be consulted?
- Can the consideration of operation and maintenance with regard to constructability improve the likely lifespan of the product and reduce the overall life cycle cost?

Considerations

The client, in association with the design leader and specialist operations and maintenance consultants, should seek to carefully consider and implement good constructability, with respect to operation and maintenance, in three key stages as follows:

First, at *the conceptual planning and design stage*:

- Design and specify for durability.
- Design and specify for reliability.
- Design and specify for longevity.
- Design and specify for maintainability.
- Design and specify for reduced life cycle costs.

Second, during *the building and/or engineering stage*:

- Supervise to avoid any compromise in the above through, for example, inadequate workmanship.

Third, during *use*, if the client is the user or occupier:

- Develop a structured approach to maintain the product in operation and use.

- Record accurately the remedial action needed to maintain the normal operating environment and account for all costs incurred.
- Provide structured feedback for detailed analysis and use in future developments.

Action

For the best possible constructability in respect of operation and maintenance, the client, design leader and appointed specialist consultants must ensure that they do the following:

- Take a life cycle view of the project where new capital projects are concerned and consider the total construction process from inception to demolition and/or replacement.
- Acquire sufficient knowledge of and ability in the project's likely life cycle, physical and cost characteristics, and ensure that these are considered early in the project's formulation.
- Incorporate the facets of durability, reliability, longevity and maintainability into the design, where it is balanced and cost-effective to do so.
- Monitor and record performance characteristics in both new projects and existing buildings to provide accurate feedback on performance and life cycle costs.

7 Constructability Case Studies

Chapters 1 to 6 have reviewed the concepts, principles and practices of constructability, reinforcing some of the principal themes with illustrative case study examples. This chapter presents a number of more detailed case studies to exemplify the contribution that constructability can make throughout the building and engineering processes. The case studies present examples in building, engineering and refurbishment work, and address some of the issues that may arise in the phases of procurement, design, engineering, construction and use. The examples reviewed cannot, of course, be held as typical of current constructability applications, but rather serve as a strong indication of the propensities of constructability in application to building and engineering processes.

Case study: 1 Multi-storey building: shaftwall construction

Background

The service cores in multi-storey buildings perform vital functions. They can be the structural spine of the building, providing support to the floors, and they are the main artery for transportation of people via lifts and fire-escape stairs. In today's high-technology, user-friendly buildings, the service core acts as a conduit for all manner of pipes, cables and communication lines.

Construction of the core is therefore becoming increasingly complex in terms of design, materials, interrelationship of the services and construction sequencing. For many multi-storey buildings, it is the speed of construction of the service core that dictates the pace of the entire project.

Designers and builders devote considerable energy to devising quicker and more efficient ways to construct these cores. Typical solutions include the following:

- precasting the core;
- jump forms of various designs;
- sliding forms for continuous pouring of concrete;
- combined steel–concrete–masonry construction where the concrete or steel structural framework is augmented by masonry that can be built later when the floors are completed.

Most solutions endeavour to speed up the construction of the core by building it more efficiently. However, a more significant solution is to break the constructional interdependency between the core and the remaining structure of the building. This is most easily achieved in steel-framed buildings, where the structural design can result in a structural form that is independent of the core. In this way the building structure can be built first, with the service core enclosure following later. Although masonry has been used in such solutions, it has the disadvantages of requiring wet trades, mass, increasing dead loads for the building, and working platforms inside the service shaft. Masonry has also succumbed to the stresses imposed by the piston effect of lift cars travelling up and down at speed, forcing the air ahead of them and against the walls of the shaft.

A plasterboard system has been developed that satisfies all these criteria. Originally developed for the steel-framed, multi-storey World Trade Centre in New York in 1968, the system has been refined and is estimated to be used in 95% of modern American high-rise office and apartment buildings. Other notable buildings using the system include the Sears Tower in Chicago and the 553-m-high CN Tower in Toronto.

The shaftwall construction system has been developed in Australia by Boral Plasterboard and used on a number of high-rise buildings, including the Southgate Tower in Adelaide and the Chifley Tower, Sydney.

Constructability

Such a solution must be introduced at conceptual stage, so that the architectural and structural design can optimise the savings. The construction stage in particular needs to adjust to the different sequencing, materials and labour requirements.

The main features are as follows:

- *Design solution*   The design of the building structure can no longer rely on the core as an integral structural component and must accommodate loads in an alternative structural form such as columns and spandrel beams. In steel-framed buildings, the weight of masonry walls around shafts is up to 219 kgf per square metre (45 lbf per square foot), creating a dead load on the structure, whereas a plasterboard system has a dead load of 75 kgf per square metre (15 lbf per square foot). A design bonus is the extra usable floor space gained because of reduced wall thickness.
- *Planning and sequencing*   Use of plasterboard shaftwall construction breaks the relationship between the construction of the core and the rest of the structure, providing the builder with greater flexibility in planning and construction.

- *Elevators*   The plasterboard enclosure is more likely to cope with the stresses imposed by the piston effect than masonry and as such is conceptualised as a 'working wall' with inherent flexibility and durability. United States practice requires that the walls resist lateral loading of 0.35 to 0.60 KPa (7.3 to 12.5 lbf/ft^2) air pressure. Since the system is non-load-bearing, alternative designs are required for the elevator doors, which need to be independently mounted. The lift car rails must span from floor to floor in order to find support.
- *Fire rating*   Fire rating requirements are achieved by firestop plasterboard, and the purpose design of channels and fixing systems to allow expansion and deflection.
- *Construction*   Shaftwall enclosures can be built once floors are completed, and can be erected from the floor without the need for provision of a working or safety platform inside the shaft. There is no need for wet trades. The full benefits are achieved when forward planning ensures that materials are ordered, delivered to site, safely stored and moved to each floor undamaged and on schedule.

Example: Southgate Tower, Adelaide, Australia

Completed in 1990, the fifteen-storey office building is of steel construction with the plasterboard shaftwall construction for the core. The stability of the structure is provided in the external moment frame, comprising columns and spandrel trusses; the structural steel perimeter columns are spaced at approximately 4.8-m centres, which enables the number of internal columns to be reduced to six, with no need for internal bracing. At lower levels, fabricated steel H - or enclosed - H sections are used with a maximum size of 460 mm 350 mm, changing to 310UCs at higher levels. The drywall-constructed core encloses the lifts, smoke exhaust, stairs and services shafts, and provides the strong physical and sound barriers as well as the fire rating. Drywall also encloses the toilet facilities.

The drywall construction is gypsum panels and light steel framing. The typical construction is two layers of 16-mm Boral Plasterboard Firestop, steel C-H studs and J-runners with 25-mm Boral Plasterboard Firestop Shaftwall liner panels (Figure 7.1).

This construction provided the equivalent sound transmission class rating of a typical masonry wall a 130 mm thick; the use of the plasterboard is much quicker than the alternative masonry, and eliminates the need for scaffolding, wet trades and rubble produced by blocklaying.

Acknowledgements

Boral plasterboard.

154

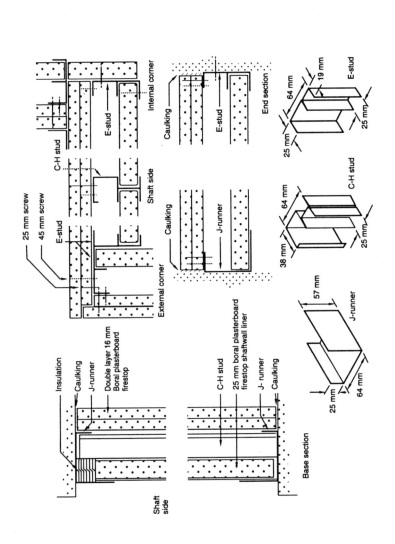

Figure 7.1   Various details of shaftwall construction in a mult-storey building (courtesy of Sidwell/Boral Plasterboard)

Case study: 2 Arts and entertainment centre: procurement

Project details

Value of project:	A$45.2 million
Client:	Premier's Department, South Australian Government
Project manager:	South Australian Department of Housing and Construction (SACON)
Architects:	Hassell Pty Ltd
Design and construction manager:	Fletcher Construction
Design start:	December 1988
Construction start:	September 1989
Handover:	Planned October 1991, Actual July 1991
Building area:	Approximately 12 000 square metres
Accommodation:	11 900 spectators

Background

The Adelaide Entertainment Centre was a state government initiative intended to enhance the social development of the state and encourage optimum tourism activity consistent with the government's economic, social and environmental objectives. The brief called for a centre capable of providing for musical, cultural and sporting events of international standards. The complex seats 11 900 spectators in a combination of fixed raked seating, retractable tiered seating, corporate boxes and area seating on the flat.

The building consists of four areas: (1) the arena area, with service areas, backstage facilities and storage; (2) loading area with workshops, toilets, food service and plant rooms; (3) corporate boxes; and (4) the foyer level with reinforced concrete post-tensioned auditorium above. External works include car parking, landscaping and roadworks. By sinking the building into the ground by some 4 m, the arena level is set at ground level, permitting easy access and reducing the overall building height.

Procurement

Registrations of interest were first called in 1985 with a local architectural practice, Hassell Pty Ltd, appointed as the principal consultants. Because this was a government project, the state government Department of Housing and Construction (SACON) acted as project managers. Detailed project design commenced in late 1988 and was developed to about 60% complete when design and construction tenders were called under a novation form of contract (Figures 7.2 and 7.3).

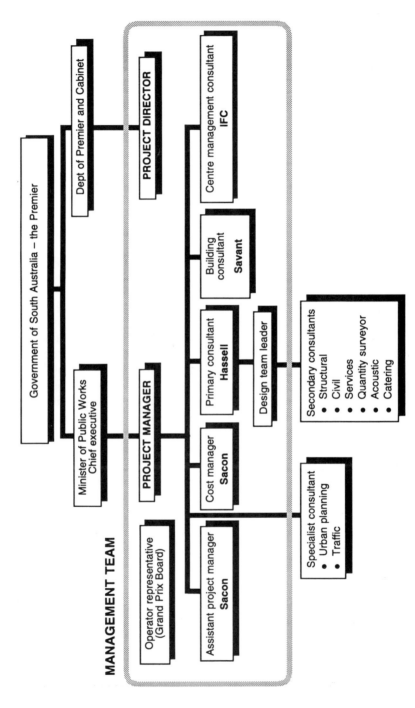

Figure 7.2   Adelaide Entertainment Centre: management team organisation for the design phase: pre-novation

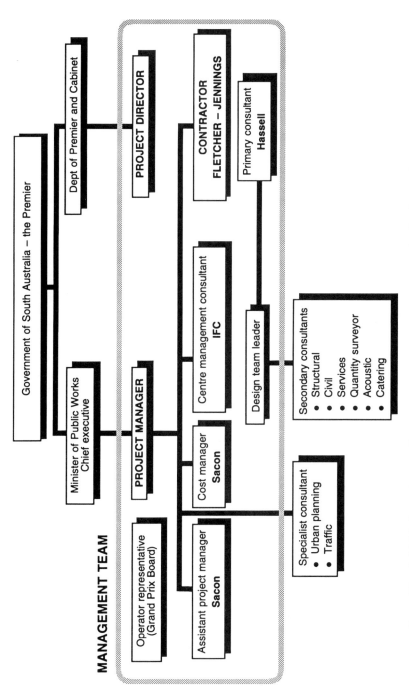

Figure 7.3   Adelaide Entertainment Centre: management team organisation for the design phase: post-novation

This project is interesting from the aspect of client involvement and acceptance of risk. From the very start, the project had the imprimatur of the premier and cabinet, who placed a high priority on its speedy and effective design and completion. The project director, a member of the premier's staff, was the main client representative, providing a clear brief, firm views on the selection of the team; the appointment of SACON as project managers and a firm budget of A$40.7 million, plus or minus 10% for the total project including demolition, fees, furniture and equipment, was approved by cabinet on 20 February 1989. (Cynical commentators have observed the parallels between the construction program and state government elections.)

Because of the tight programme and budget, the project managers recommended a novation form of contract. The principal architectural consultants were appointed to develop the design up to the point of novation, they engaged their own sub-consultants. The project managers engaged a building consultant to help with constructability and planning.

Tenders were called on a fixed, lump-sum basis, with no provision for rise and fall based on the usual Australian standard conditions of contract 'General Conditions of Contract NPWC 3 (1981)', with some special conditions of contract and annexures. Tenderers were at liberty to submit alternative proposals and had to provide details of the manner by which the principal consultant was to be engaged, once the contract was novated. The special conditions included clauses relating to performance requirements, responsibilities assumed by the builder, agreement with the principal consultant, variations, the recovery of claims, and industrial relations. A schedule of indicative bulk quantities was included, but was not guaranteed as accurate.

Tenders were called from five large building companies on 17 July 1989, and the bids received on 25 August ranged from A$44.5 million to A$55 million, compared with a building budget of A$37.5 million, a range of between 18 and 45% over budget. Negotiations were entered into with the lowest bidder.

Constructability challenges

There were a number of challenging issues, which were tackled and solved by goodwill and co-operation between the team members. Some of these were constructability issues and others illustrate the importance of co-operation. Savings of A$4 million were negotiated, bringing the tender within the 10% margin set by the cabinet.

- *Industrial relations and wet weather*   The fixed price contract did not allow for extensions of time due to industrial disputes (other than state-wide or national disputes) or wet weather, and tenderers were clearly pricing for this risk. Liquidated damages were heavy, owing to potential losses if planned entertainment events had to be cancelled. The industrial relations climate in Australia is aggressive, with high-profile projects frequently the target of disputation. In the event, the project escaped major disputation, however at the start a reduction of the margin for risk was achieved by the client agreeing to share the risk by allowing a thirty day period of grace without penalty.

- *Ground conditions*   The site was thought to be poor ground. The project manager undertook exploratory excavations to allay the apprehensions of the contractor.
- *Design and specifications*   The lowest bidder opened the books to identify the high-cost components and explore the opportunities for savings. A range of modifications were made to the design and specifications.
- *Subcontractors' prices*   With the risks more sharply in focus, the contractor was able to renegotiate prices with subcontractors.
- *Roof construction*   The roof structure was a major construction challenge. The rectangular building is 142 m long by 90 m wide. The roof structure was of eight primary space frame steel trusses, each weighing 27 tonne and spanning 85 m between 10 m to 20 m above slab level. The roof covering is colour-coated steel sheeting with insulation.

The builder could not assemble the roof at ground level and lift the roof structure up by crane, because this would be too expensive. The unions would have insisted on a fully boarded working platform if construction were *in situ*. Over the total area, this would have cost in the region of A$1 million. The final innovative, constructible solution was a combination of crane lifts for the trusses, with a specially fabricated working cage suspended by crane for fixing the roof sheeting. Detailed work routines, maintaining full safety precautions, had to be hammered out with site labour.

Acknowledgements:

Judy Freeman, Assistant Project Manager, SACON;
Peter Salveston, Project Manager, Fletcher Construction.

Case study 3: Reservoir and pumping station

Background

This case study describes the engineering of a brine reservoir and pumping station for a major petrochemical industry organisation. Interest focuses upon the method and sequence of excavation and haul of bulk spoil from the reservoir earthworks. The site itself was relatively uncomplicated, being a green-field development, but the local planning authority had demanded as part of its environmental assessment procedures that the natural sheltering belt of trees and vegetation to the site should be retained and further improved. This served as a major influence on the consideration given to constructability in the project.

Constructability

Figure 7.4 illustrates the layout and section through the brine reservoir and pumping station. The plan shows how the engineering earthworks were carried out by excavating three main swathes from the perimeter of the slope top to the centre of the reservoir dig. This enabled the contractor to schedule a sequence of operations simultaneously in each of the three swathes. On similar projects previously carried out, the contractor had worked from an earthworks basis of one or two swathes, but not three synchronised digs. It was seen that the multi-swathe approach worked well, allowing motor-scrapers efficient access onto and from the dig in a one-way traffic management pattern. Scrapers and hauling trucks were managed to a predetermined mass-haul schedule to encourage efficient and effective utilisation and moreover, they were timed onto the site to ensure that there were no traffic tailbacks during waits for the loading of spoil materials.

The environmental aspect was recognised in the layout of the earthworks. It can seen in the layout diagram that the construction accesses to the earthworks were determined to coincide with the natural topography and existing tree belt. This formation ensured that there was minimal disruption to existing features and necessitated the minimum of new tree planting to reinstate the sheltering of the site from the surrounding environs.

The excavations for the brine mains are of considerable interest. Detailed site investigation of the subsoil conditions along the intended dig revealed a considerable number of short stretches where running sand and other naturally unstable materials were present. Once the exact position and length of those conditions was determined, interlocking steel sheet piling was introduced, but with novel application. A prefabricated timber jig was used to quickly position sheeting on both sides of the trench in an accurate way. This was essential to speed up the excavating process, but also, moreover, to ensure that the piling insertion avoided the presence of existing pipework sited very close to the new brine mains.

Case study 4: Academic facility: steel framed system building

Background

This case study concerns the application of site constructability to a steel-framed system-built project. The building had an approximate total floor area of 5 000 square metres provided in a ground floor plus two-storey steel portal

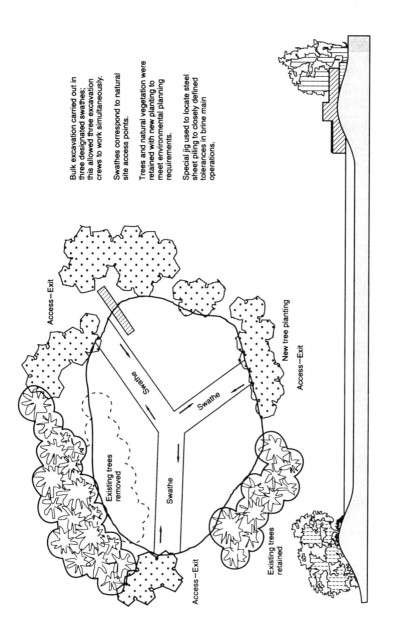

Bulk excavation carried out in three designated swathes; this allowed three excavation crews to work simultaneously.

Swathes correspond to natural site access points.

Trees and natural vegetation were retained with new planting to meet environmental planning requirements.

Special jig used to locate steel sheet piling to closely defined tolerances in brine main operations.

Access—Exit

New tree planting

Access—Exit

Swathe

Swathe

Swathe

Swathe

Existing trees removed

Access—Exit

Existing trees retained

Figure 7.4   Illustrative layout and section for the construction of a reservoir and pumping station

frame design. The frame was built on a variable-depth reinforced concrete slab set on piled, pad and beam foundations. The principal superstructure enclosure materials were rustic facing bricks to the north elevation and a specially designed high-specification cladding to the remaining elevations and the roof structure. The works also comprised extensive external works, drainage, landscaping and the provision of car parking around the building. The general layout and elevations are shown in Figures 7.5 to 7.8.

Constructability

The focus of constructability consideration on this project was directed towards *site constructability,* although some aspects of design constructability were also addressed.

In consciously striving to apply constructability principles to the project the contractor sought to:

- Examine the designer's conceptualisation of the construction elements not in terms of their design constituents but in their implications to the practical construction requirements.
- Determine the optimum organisation and site layout to undertake the required operations and tasks, promoting innovative techniques and accessibility where possible.
- Anticipate the effects of the design requirement upon trade constitution to promote better skills and teamwork and encourage greater site performance.

Application

If we refer to the building's layout and elevation drawings it can be seen how the principal areas for consideration were applied.

Site layout and organisation

Accessibility to and around the site was given priority by the contractor in assisting good site constructability.

Site access

Access to the site was carefully considered to avoid hindrance to the existing main road and access roads around the development. One access point was utilised throughout. It was consciously determined that there would be free access around the proposed building, and to this end the location of site hutting, permanent plant and storage of materials was not permitted directly around the perimeter of the building.

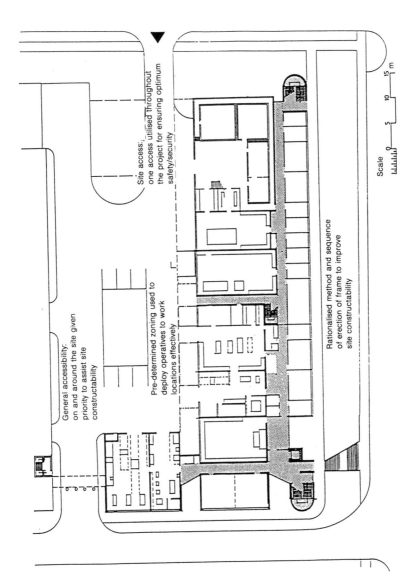

Site access:
one access utilised throughout
the project for ensuring optimum
safety/security

General accessibility:
on and around the site given
priority to assist site
constructability

Pre-determined zoning used to
deploy operatives to work
locations effectively

Rationalised method and sequence
of erection of frame to improve
site constructability

Scale

0   5   10   15 m

Figure 7.5   Steel-framed system build project: ground-floor plan

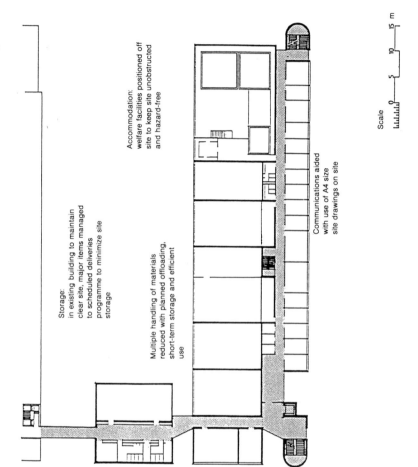

Storage:
in existing building to maintain
clear site, major items managed
to scheduled deliveries
programme to minimize site
storage

Multiple handling of materials
reduced with planned offloading,
short-term storage and efficient
use

Accommodation:
welfare facilities positioned off
site to keep site unobstructed
and hazard-free

Communications aided
with use of A4 size
site drawings on site

Scale

0   5   10   15 m

Figure 7.6   Steel-framed system build project: first-floor plan

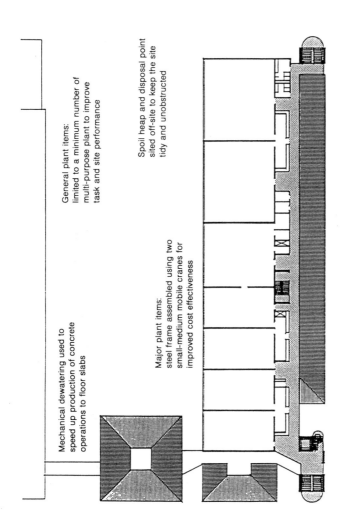

Mechanical dewatering used to speed up production of concrete operations to floor slabs

General plant items: limited to a minimum number of multi-purpose plant to improve task and site performance

Spoil heap and disposal point sited off-site to keep the site tidy and unobstructed

Major plant items: steel frame assembled using two small-medium mobile cranes for improved cost effectiveness

Scale

0   5   10   15 m

Figure 7.7   Steel-framed system build project: second-floor plan

166

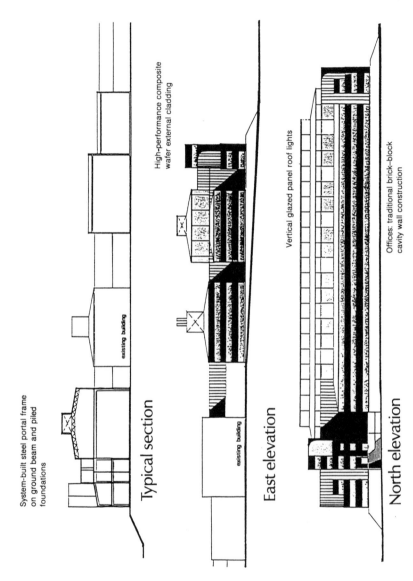

System-built steel portal frame on ground beam and piled foundations

existing building

Typical section

High-performance composite wafer external cladding

existing building

East elevation

Vertical glazed panel roof lights

Offices: traditional brick–block cavity wall construction

North elevation

Figure 7.8 *Steel-framed system build project: elevations*

Movement on site

The vacant site space between the proposed development and the existing buildings to the southern aspect was left unoccupied to allow open construction access. It was predetermined that there would be sufficient space to allow the largest scheduled plant items (cranes) to work and move freely according to programme.

Accommodation and welfare facilities

All site accommodation, meeting current health and welfare regulations, were positioned to a self-contained hardstanding area to the south-west of the proposed development, again ensuring that the site remained unobstructed.

Additional facilities

Arrangements with the client allowed the use of sanitary and other conveniences within existing buildings during site working hours. This removed the need for personal facilities to be placed directly at the workplace.

Operational control

As part of a programme of planned operational control, the contractor considered the effects of the following site aspects upon constructability:

Construction plant and equipment

Allocated construction plant was limited to a minimum number of major items. These were selected to be multi-purpose rather than specialist, which, it was felt, would improve general task and site performance. Specific attention was given to crane selection in the movement and assembly of the steel frame.

Storage and handling of materials

- The contractor compiled a schedule of the main construction materials and components required and their storage requirements. This was carefully considered relative to the construction programme, and it was determined that the construction sequence allowed limited but multi-purpose storage and handling to be adopted. For example, because concreting could take place early in the programme the assigned areas for fabricating and storing formwork and reinforcement could be converted to storage and cutting of blockwork, and later still the pre-assembly of cladding components. In this way locations for delivery, storage, fabrication and handling could be minimised, so alleviating multiple handling operations.

- The contractor obtained the consent of the client to store materials and components in the existing buildings to the southern part of the site. This allowed the easier delivery and storage of vulnerable components, and provided a secure store for valuable fixtures and fittings later in the contract.
- Programmed delivery schedules were compiled for the main structural components: ready-mixed concrete, steel frame members, cladding and roof sheetings, and roller-shutter door sets. This eliminated the problems of bulk storage and handling on site.

Spoil heap and disposal points

A designated spoil heap and disposal point was positioned on a vacant plot to the south of the site accommodation area. This centralised disposal point allowed the site to remain tidy and unobstructed, and also prevented any potential safety hazard around the existing development.

Techniques of assembly

Steel frame assembly and superstructure enclosure

Much of the reasoning for maintaining a clear and unobstructed site concerned the need for handling, positioning and assembly of the steel-framed elements. While previous individual projects on the development site saw contractors utilising a tower crane, the contractor on this project site determined that it would be more innovative and cost-effective to employ two small-medium sized mobile cranes, which could operate all round the site, assisting in cladding and roofing operations in addition to the assembly of the steelwork.

Concreting works

The reinforced concrete ground floor slab was designed to be cast in the optimum width of bays permissible, utilising steel edge forms which could be moved to subsequent casting bays. An innovative feature of the concreting operations saw the use of mechanical dewatering plant to speed up production and finishing of the ground floor operations.

Case study 5: Multi-storey building services: Fast Track lift installation

Background

A Melbourne team has designed a revolutionary way of combining lift installation with the jump form construction of service cores for multi-storey reinforced-concrete buildings. When the core is completed, the lifts can be quickly brought into commission, thus saving time later and providing superior access for site personnel and materials throughout the remainder of the construction.

Traditional lift installation

The traditional method of lift installation commences once the core is complete and the contractor has given possession of the lift shafts. The installer must work from temporary platforms, lifting materials such as rails, trimmer beams, door frames, etc., by winch or block and tackle up the lift shaft. Progress is slow and inefficient, owing to restricted working space, manhandling of components and the constant need to move the working platform up the shaft. The work method is also hazardous, and particular attention is required to safety.

Lift installation is usually on the critical path, and therefore contributes to the overall duration of the project. because final commissioning of the lift does not usually occur until well into the project, the builder is denied the opportunity to utilise the lift for transportation and must provide temporary hoisting and passenger facilities. These are generally linked to the construction of the superstructure and require extending periodically. There is inefficiency both when the temporary lift does not reach all the floors and when it is unavailable owing to its being extended.

Fast Track lift installation

The Fast Track system consists of a number of laser-aligned trailing decks and platforms suspended from the Lubeca hydraulic jump form system. These additional decks hang below the jump form within the multiple lift shaft. The suspended deck has a steel floor, which is also a template for each lift. Slots are provided in the floor to allow the deck to pass over the rails, conduits, etc., that project through.

This deck provides a more safe and accessible working environment. Access is usually by means of a personnel and materials hoist installed in one of the lift shafts.

Because the installation is carried out on a level by level basis – dictated by each 'jump' of the jump form – all the components for the lifts have to be manufactured to suit. Packs of materials are made up in the factory: each set of rails, trimmer beams, lift doors, door frames, etc., is made up and packed precisely to suit the installation team on site. Final installation operations are performed in the conventional manner for machine room fit out, car super-structure and counterweight installation and final tuning (Figure 7.9).

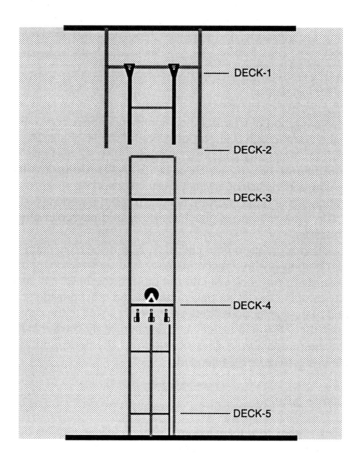

Figure 7.9   *Detail of a fast track lift installation in a multi-storey building (courtesy of Sidwell/Boral Elevators). This vertical schematic of one of the 4 banks shows the builder's climb-form superstructure. Deck 1 is the top work area where concrete is poured. Decks 2 and 3 are for the climb form workers to set panels, steel reinforcing, prepared openings, and so on. The new feature is the addition of Decks 4 and 5 for the lift installer suspended by steel pipes from the upper decks. Each time the climb form jumps one floor, Decks 4 and 5 rise with it.*

Constructability advantages

A leading firm of quantity surveyors has estimated the savings and other benefits as follows:

- The lift installation team must work at the same pace as the jump form construction team. On projects completed so far, this has not caused any difficulties.
- The lift installation is removed from the critical path, being completed much earlier in the project, allowing the builder to use the lifts for personnel and materials. This is much more efficient than relying on the traditional builders' hoists. By coming on stream earlier, the lifts provide transportation during the period of peak activity and manning levels on site.

On the basis of experience on early projects and computer modelling, the quantity surveyors estimate that savings in waiting time, journey time and materials handling bring an increase in productivity that can reduce the overall programme for a typical high-rise building by four weeks.

This earlier completion time brings savings in preliminaries and holding charges, and enhanced income due to earlier completion for the building owner.

- The system is more tightly programmed, with more of the prefabrication carried out off site in the factory, resulting in better quality control.
- The working decks provide a safer, more accessible and better-lit environment, which is likely to enhance labour productivity and reduce the likelihood of industrial disputation.

The computer model was based on a typical high-rise building of 27 levels and 3 basement levels, costing A\$270 million, a total construction period of 144 weeks or 720 working days, with an average total labour force of 330 peaking at about 500.

The Fast Track system brings the lift installation on stream at day 340, with the full effect of improved personnel transport to all floors occurring from day 450. The estimated time saving on the project is four weeks and a cost saving of A\$5 million.

Acknowledgement

Mr Brian McKenzie, Boral Elevators
Melbourne, Victoria.

Case study 6: Historic building refurbishment

Background

This case study concerns the complete refurbishment of a historically signifi-cant office building sited within a booming city-centre business locale. Whereas the original layout of the building divided the available usable space into small individual offices, a modern interior was created on six floors to an open-plan design. This meant that the usable floor space could serve as a complete office complex or be occupied on a floor-by-floor basis. The ground and lower ground floor levels were designed as a distinctive, high-quality commercial facility, but developed as a separate entity in such a way that its use would not impinge upon the upper level offices (Figure 7.10). The local planning authority demanded that the external facade should be retained in its existing form and be upgraded with repair and stone cleaning as required for a building with historic significance, but allowed the design team to remodel the interior layout as seen fit.

Constructability

The design team proposed to tear out the interior, leaving only the external walls and then to reinstate the interior using modern techniques and materi-als to create the high-quality, purpose-built commercial and office facility.

Interior construction works required the removal of all floors, internal partitions and the roof structure, leaving only the structural frame. To support the remaining frame, the contractor utilised a purpose-built steel bracing system that could be progressively installed as the demolition works pro-ceeded from the roof downwards. This assisted the demolition works con-siderably, making good time and cost savings achievable.

In constructing the ground and intermediate floors metal-decked access flooring was used. This facilitated built-in duct channelling in which modern electronic systems cabling could be installed easily and quickly during fitting out. Again, this was a positive contribution to enhancing constructability not only during the construction phase but during occupation and use.

The project, completed five weeks within the envisaged eighteen-month timescale and with a 4 per cent cost saving, represented a useful example of the way in which an old but structurally sound building could be adapted to meet modern city-centre requirements.

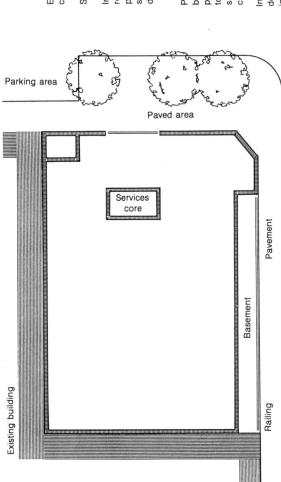

External façade retained, cleaned and repaired

Structural shell retained

Internal walls, floors and roof removed utilising purpose designed structural support system during demolition

Progressively installing the steel bracing system as demolition proceeded downward from roof to ground influenced a time saving of 5 weeks and a 4-per-cent saving on cost

Intermediate floors utilised metal decked access flooring to incorporate duct channelling for electronic systems cabling

Parking area

Paved area

Services core

Existing building

Basement

Pavement

Railing

NTS

Figure 7.10   Illustrative layout of historic building refurbishment project

Case study 7: Local government publice service building: low-rise traditional construction

Background

This case study concerns the application of design constructability to a local government authority low-rise traditional building project. The building, approximately 1 000 m^2 in usable floor area, had the main accommodation on the ground floor, with a small upper storey section. A traditional design solution determined that the ground floor and foundation construction should comprise a reinforced *in situ* concrete slab with a variable-depth, downstand perimeter mass concrete beam. The superstructure incorporated a single-leaf concrete block wall with external rendering and a timber-decked roof structure finished with felt covering. The upper storey section comprised lightweight prefabricated panels supported by an *in situ* reinforced concrete slab, again finished with timber decking and bituminous coverings. Internal walls comprised timber stud partitioning finished with dry linings and plaster skim. Building services consisted of a gas-fired hot water heating system and partial mechanical ventilation system to predetermined parts of the building. There were also extensive external works, drainage, landscaping and general site works. Figures 7.11 to 7.13 depict the general layout and elevations of the building.

Constructability

Constructability consideration by the design team extended to the following principal aspects:

- standardisation;
- simplification;
- technical and modular co-ordination.

Standardisation

Standardisation is concerned with promoting the repetition of technical construction details and use of designs that allow repetitive or similar building layouts.

Standardisation in design is intrinsically inhibited by complex building elevations. Returns and recesses in the perimeter walling make both design and construction continuity problematic. It can be seen that standardisation in the design of some external wall elevations makes the design and construction easier to undertake, integrating the team skills of the bricklaying and joinery trades.

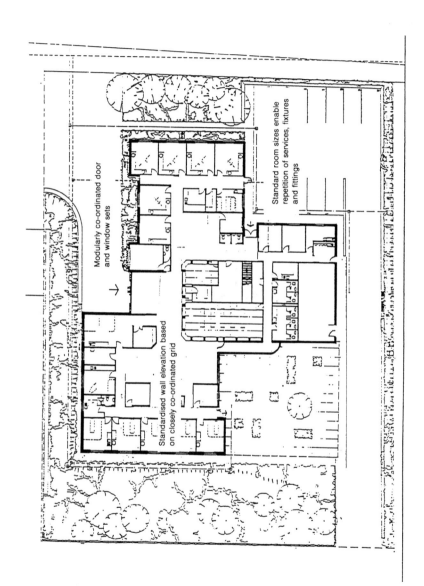

Modularly co-ordinated door and window sets

Standardised wall elevation based on closely co-ordinated grid

Standard room sizes enable repetition of services, fixtures and fittings

Figure 7.11   Public service building: ground-floor plan

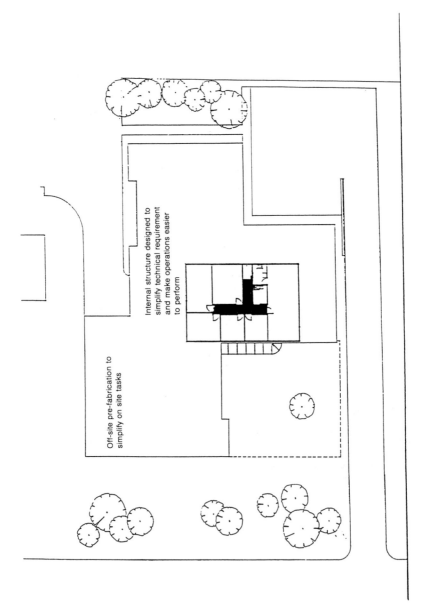

Off-site pre-fabrication to simplify on site tasks

Internal structure designed to simplify technical requirement and make operations easier to perform

Figure 7.12   Public service building: first-floor plan

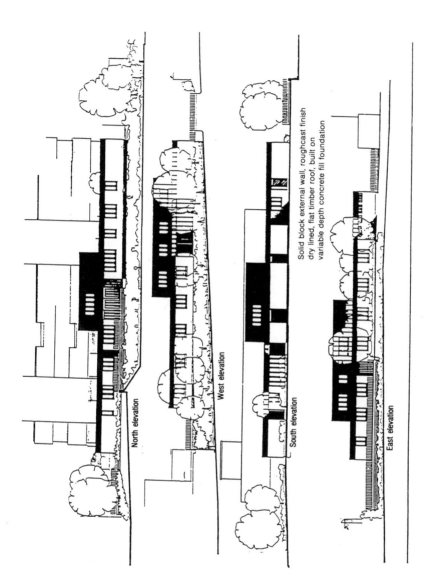

North elevation

West elevation

South elevation

East elevation

Solid block external wall, roughcast finish
dry lined, flat timber roof, built on
variable depth concrete fill foundation

Figure 7.13   Public service building: elevations

Continuing on the theme of standardisation, the internal layout was designed to incorporate standard room sizes where possible. This allowed the repetition of many design features and construction tasks. Examples of this include the specification of standard door sets, common service installations and fixture and fitting kits.

Simplification

Simplification of design detail and construction tasks aims to simplify the technical requirements and make construction operations easier to undertake on site, without detracting from the building's desired specification or performance.

Simplification could be seen in the designer's use of lightweight, internal timber stud partitions. These were incorporated as the principal space-dividing medium within the layout, and linking in with standardisation allowed for the specification of standard door sets, common coverings and finishes.

Within the roofing design, joist hangers were adopted to simplify the technical detail. This was achieved as their use eliminated an otherwise necessary return to the construction element by the bricklaying gang. Building-in the ends of the joists not only requires return visits to the workplace but is very time-consuming.

A further example of simplification was seen in the siting of electrical, gas, water and other essential services to the building. These were designed to be incorporated as an integral part of the floor construction method.

Technical and modular co-ordination

Constructability can invariably suffer where different design elements or construction methods interface. Technical and modular co-ordination seeks to eliminate such difficulties by closely intermeshing ostensibly different design elements and the construction tasks involved.

The design sought to use technical and modularly co-ordinated window sets, where all building elevations had the same type, style and size of windows. With these linked-in to the elevation blockwork laying and cutting details, the difficulties of building-in the sets were minimised.

Modular co-ordination in the roofing element saw the designer co- ordinate timber joists and boardings in such a way that most could be revised and cut off-site and be delivered to their final fix position almost in kit assembly form. This clearly assisted in improving task accessibility at the workplace, as fabrication was eliminated and assembly assisted.

8 Constructability: An Overview

The concept of constructability, or buildability as it is called in the UK, although buildability defines a more specific concept now accepted as being part of constructability emerged in the late 1970s as a result of research into cost efficiency and quality in the construction industry. The separation of the design and construction processes, which was partly due to traditional contractual procedures, was cited as the major factor hindering constructability, resulting in budgets being exceeded and deadlines being overrun.

Considerable research into constructability concepts has been conducted over many years and in many countries. In the UK research was narrowly focused, highlighting techniques and details, with an emphasis on improving productivity by design rationalisation. Unlike in the US, there was not the emphasis on management systems and the involvement of owners and contractors. These factors, together with the separation of inputs in the traditional building process, led to a lack of general interest in constructability concepts in the UK. In the US however, constructability has been followed with some vigour and with greater enthusiasm within the construction industry. The US approach, led by the Construction Industry Institute (CII), capitalises on the close link between owners and contractors and emphasising a management system to generate creativity and thought about the construction process.

Similarly, the Construction Industry Institute (CII) in Australia adopted a management-based approach to constructability, generating the constructability principles file. The Principles File represents the best in current constructability practice and is aimed at encouraging a project team to apply wholly practical measures to improve the construction processes. Such an implementational method focuses on key issues, rather than specific procedures, to allow for variations in organisational cultures and practices, thus broadening the potential application of the concepts of constructability.

The size of a construction project, or indeed organisation, should never be perceived as a barrier to the implementation of constructability. The concepts and principles of constructability are equally applicable to both large and small organisations, and should in practice be tailored to the particular type of project. Although it is not possible to determine a single approach that would be appropriate to every organisation or project, there are common elements in all situations upon which a sound constructability approach can be developed for any one of them.

There is little doubt that constructability is more successful when its concepts and principles become an inherent and accepted part of the way a project is conceived and organised. For benefits to be maximised therefore, the project team, led by the client, must have a corporate policy on constructability. This must be reinforced by a constructability programme, and this must become a part of the project process from the feasibility stage onwards and be suited to the contractual format adopted. Constructability is most effective when the project team endorses and implements its concepts because of the real benefits that it can bring to the project rather than by merely following procedures.

It has been clearly shown in this book that constructability is a concept that transcends the total construction process. Constructability has an important role to play in conceptual planning, design and engineering, procurement and construction, and in use. The timing of the implementation of thinking on constructability is crucial to its success, because the ability to influence cost is greatest during the initial stages of a building or engineering project. The application of thinking on constructability as early as possible in the project sequence will therefore enhance practical and financial benefits.

Three other factors are highly significant to the successful implementation of constructability: first, the conscious will of the client to pursue the concepts of constructability; second, the early involvement of construction personnel to contribute practical constructability expertise; third, and perhaps most important, the highest level of commitment by all participants to the total construction process.

As with so many aspects of construction management, only with thorough and professional application will constructability achieve success and receive the due recognition that it deserves as a significant contributor to the advancement of the construction process.

Appendix   Glossary of Terms

This appendix presents the definition of terms relevant to this work. Where referenced, definitions are derived from authoritative sources.

buildability   The extent to which the design of a building facilitates ease of construction, subject to the overall requirements for the completed building. (Construction Industry Research and Information Association)

constructability   A system for achieving optimum integration of construction knowledge in the building process and balancing the various project and environmental constraints to achiev maximisation of project goals and building performance. (Construction Industry Institute, Australia)

construction management contract   This contract is similar to a management contract except that the client is the employer in each works construction contract. (A. Turner, *Building Procurement*, Macmillan, London, 1990)

contractor's proposals   Within a design–build contract, proposals made by a contractor for the design and construction of a building or other structure.

design and manage   A form of building procurement whereby the contractor is responsible for the design and the management of the construction of the works undertaken by a series of works contractors. (D. E. L. Janssens, *Design-Build Explained*, Macmillan, London, 1991)

design–build   A form of building procurement whereby the contractor who constructs the works, also undertakes all of, or a proportion of, the design of the works. (D. E. L. Janssens, *Design-Build Explained*, Macmillan, London, 1991)

employer's requirements   A statement of the client's requirements when inviting tenders for a design–build contract, or any other form of contract!

management contract   This is a contract in which management is regarded as a separate discipline and responsibility from that of construction . . . . Construction (works) contractors contract with a management contractor, who is therefore their client or employer. (A. Turner, *Building Procurement*, Macmillan, London, 1990)

novation   A hybrid variation of design–build procurement where the client appoints a designer (architect) to develop a concept design and passes on that designer to the contractor.

project management   The overall planning, control and co-ordination of a project from inception to completion aimed at meeting a client's requirements and ensuring completion on time, within cost and to the required quality standards. (Chartered Institute of Building)

traditional contracting   A method of building procurement, where responsibility for the design lies with the client's (employer's) consultant and a contractor is responsible for the construction.

works contract   A contractor who carries out construction work under a management contract or construction management arrangement. (A. Turner, *Building Procurement* Macmillan, London, 1990)

Select Bibliography

The following references present detailed research material encapsulating buildability and constructability.

S. Adams, *Practical Buildability*, CIRIA/Butterworth, London, 1989.

K. Allsopp, 'Buildability: An Architect's View' (1983) *Architects Journal*, vol. 177 (1983) no. 5.

A. Baxter, 'Buildability: A Structural Engineer's View (1983) *Architects Journal*, vol. 177 (1983) no. 5.

D. Bishop, *Buildability: Whose Responsibility?*, Paper, Buildability Conference, Barbican Centre, London, 1983.

Construction Industry Institute (CII), Australia, *Constructability Principles File*, CII, University of South Australia, 1993.

Construction Industry Research and Information Association (CIRIA), *Buildability: An Assessment*, CIRIA Publications, London 1983, Special Publication no. 26.

I. Ferguson, *Buildability in Practice* Mitchell, London, 1989.

A. Griffith, *Buildability: The Effect of Design and Management on Construction*, SERC/Heriot-Watt University Publication, Edinburgh, 1985.

A. Griffith, 'Buildability: A Time for Reassessment', *Building Technology and Management* (1988).

M. Hatchett, 'Buildability: A Teacher's View', *Architects Journal*, vol. 177 (1983) no. 9.

J. R. Illingworth, 'Buildability — Tomorrow's Need', *Building Technology and Management* (1984)

F. P. McDermott, 'Buildability: Delays and Disruptions to Construction Sequence', SERC Report, 1986, unpublished

W. S. MacLachlan and C. Mansfield, 'Buildability: A Contractor's View', *Architects Journal*, vol. 177, (1983) no. 7.

National Economic Development Office (NEDO), *Achieving Quality on Building Sites*, HMSO, London, 1987.

J. J. O'Connor and R. L. Tucker, 'Improving Industrial Project Constructability', PhD Thesis, University of Texas, 1983, unpublished.

O. Osman, 'The Modelling of Factors Influencing Observed Manpower Productive Time within the Site Production Process', PhD Thesis, Heriot-Watt University, Edinburgh, 1989, unpublished.

M. Powell, 'Buildability: A Researcher's View', *Architects Journal*, vol. 177 (1983) no. 10.

G. Ridout, 'Designers Must Bear the Blame for Poor Buildability', *Contract Journal* (1983) (March).

J. Warren, 'Buildability: A Report's Review', *Architects Journal*, vol. 177 (1983) no. 13.

B. Williams, 'Buildability: A Quantity Surveyor's View', *Architects Journal*, vol.177 (1983) no. 6.

Index

accessibility   17, 19, 21, 85, 107, 117
American Society of Civil Engineers
      (ASCE)   13
available resources   21, 107, 120
awareness   4, 40

barriers to implementation   26, 31, 62
benefits   25, 68
briefing   38, 44
buildability   6
   concepts   7
   guidelines   7
   research studies   7
building process   1, 42

client requirements   42
client's agent   50
climatic conditions   18
   access   17
   dry working   17
   securing work areas   17
   service penetration   17
collaboration   5
commissioning   138
communication   5, 40, 51, 107, 120
conceptual planning   23, 24, 35, 42
constructability   1, 17, 85, 106
   concepts   1, 11, 19
   principles   1, 16, 22, 40
Construction Industry Institute (CII)   2,
      10, 13, 18
Construction Industry Research and
      Information Association (CIRIA)   6
construction innovation   21, 107
construction knowledge   21, 107
construction management   10, 19, 35,
      50
   industrial relations   15, 17
   managerial style   32, 35
   material procurement   32
   methods of planning   10, 124

operational planning and control   11,
      21, 32
   organisational structure   11
   safety   17, 119
   use of plant   11
construction methodology   21, 35
corporate objectives   21, 45

definitions   181
design   3, 17, 23, 35, 38, 85, 106
   complexity   86, 110
   concepts   7
   details   17, 107
   evaluation   86, 107, 110
   layout   86, 107, 115
   maintenance   33, 138, 143
   materials   86, 109
   operational requirements   86, 107,
      122
   quality   58, 72
   rationalisation   6, 86, 110
   services   18, 98
   workplaces   86, 107
design and construct   46
dimensional co-ordination   86

economic objectives   1, 43
education   27, 40
employee relations   17, 126
   contractor performance   17, 107, 124
   enterprise agreements   17
   industrial relations   16, 17
   mixed trades   15, 126
   multi-skilling   117, 107, 127
   number of trades   17
   sequencing   17
examples   87, 128, 151
   construction   128, 151
   design   87, 151
external factors   6
   climate   18

external factors (*cont.*)
  economic   43
  environmental   18
  regulatory   17, 118

feasibility   37
  stage   37
feedback   21, 24
  concepts   21
  loops   21
  mechanisms   21

incentives   17, 126
  bonus schemes   16, 126
integration   3, 64
  client-design   64, 74
  client-contractor   64, 74
  contractor-designer   64, 74
  consultants   64, 74

maintenance   33, 138
  strategies   138
  repairs   138, 143
  requirements   138
management-based methods   64, 74
  construction management   64
  management contracting   64
management: design-based   64, 74
  consultant-based project
    management   64
  contractor-based project
    management   64
management systems   64, 114
material fabrication   86
modular co-ordination   86

National Economic Development Office
    (NEDO)   6, 31
new assets   139
  management   139
  strategies   139

personnel   107
  organisation   107, 113, 115
  selection   126
  skills   107, 126
  training   126
planning   124, 125

prefabrication   112
principles (constructability) file   19
priorities   2, 27
  client   2, 4
  construction   2
procurement   18, 44
  contracts   64, 74
  delivery systems   44, 64, 74
  non-traditional   44, 45, 64
  novation   61
  risk analysis   18
  selection   44
  traditional   44, 45
post-construction phase   24, 138
productivity   32, 107, 124
production methods   11, 85
  construction knowledge   108
  deployment of resources   108
  method of construction   85
  method of site management   108
  sequence of assembly   108, 111, 125
  standards   107
professional advisers   49
professional demarcation   27, 47
programme   45, 124
project characteristics   10, 17, 106
  availability of resources   17, 107, 120
  location of site   17, 120
  regulations   17, 117
  restrictions   17, 117, 118
  site conditions   17, 120
  size of site   17, 115
  type of construction   17, 111

qualified personnel   14, 28, 113
quality   58, 72

regional/situational factors   35, 36
reporting   21
  feedback   21, 24
  loops   21, 24
  mechanisms   21, 24

safety   17, 119
  code requirements   17
  maintenance   33, 138
  measures   17
simplification   110

site factors   106, 115
   access   117
   egress   117
   geotechnical   17
   materials   109, 120
   physical features   17
   weather   17
   workforce   17, 107
   workspace   17, 107
specifications   8, 17, 85
standardisation   15, 17
strategies   40

team skills   8, 17, 85
technical co-ordination   17
tendering   38

time management   58

uncertainty   46
   price   49
   project   42
use   36, 138, 143
use of building   138, 143
   installation and commissioning   138
   operational requirements   138, 143
   preventive maintenance   142
   reactive maintenance   145

value for money   43, 60

wastage on site   118